MW01640154

Spotlight on History

Hugh Chase

Compiled by: Michael Chase

A division of Squire Publishers, Inc.
4500 College Blvd.
Leawood, KS 66211
1/888/888-7696

Printed in the United States

ISBN: 1-58597-146-4

Library of Congress Control Number: 2002106810

A division of Squire Publishers, Inc.
4500 College Blvd.
Leawood, KS 66211
1/888/888-7696

Dedication

To all the Police Officers past, present and future of the Kansas City Police Department who put their lives in jeopardy every day protecting the citizens of Kansas City.

TABLE OF CONTENTS

FOREWORD

Hugh Chase, a Kansas City, Missouri Police Officer injured in the line of duty, became the Police Department's historian from 1960 through 1982. During this stint, his love for the history of Kansas City and its Police Department was reflected in a series of articles featured in the publications, "K.C. Police News," "The Informant" and "The Baton." His by-line was "Spotlight on History." He was also a published writer in many detective magazines.

Hugh Chase's vignettes give humorous, but factual, reviews of the life and times of Kansas City, Missouri's Police Department. These stories were a labor of love for my dad, his "Spotlight on History."

WEST BOTTOMS

OVER A CENTURY AGO, Francois Chouteau sailed up the Missouri River, arriving where it joins with the Kansas (Kaw) River. This area was ideal for fur trapping and possessed the natural conditions required for a settlement. The confluence of the Missouri and Kaw Rivers had produced a lush virgin forest, rich in berries and game. If Chouteau made the journey today and viewed this same land, he would sail on without hesitation.

Throughout its history, this region has been known as the French Bottoms, West Kansas, the West Bottoms, and the Central Industrial District. The moment Chouteau set foot on the south bank of the Missouri River, Kansas City's illustrious evolvement began.

The Bottoms was a natural valley at the junction of the two rivers. The region became the hub for packinghouse companies, quickly putting Kansas City on the map. From the time of Francois Chouteau, the area became an active trading center for trappers, hunters, farmers and Indians. Six years after the Civil War ended, founding of the stockyards quickly became a symbol of the growth that characterized the region. It began modestly on a thirteen-and-a-half-acre tract and eventually created a centrally marked place for western livestock. This interest quickly elevated Kansas City to a prime trading center.

The district was a town unto itself in the final decade of the nineteenth century. Residential areas sprang up south

Figure 1 — Flood in West Bottoms, ca. 1893
Photo: Kansas City Library Photographs

of Twelfth Street, with an estimated population of five thousand. This population consisted mainly of workers employed in the Bottoms. Residents living on the bluff snubbed those living in the Bottoms and social contact was limited between the factions. This was due in part to the forty-five minutes travel by mule train between the two points.

Adventurers lured to the West to make a fortune struck it rich in the growing activity north of Twelfth Street. Garrett Fleming, a saloonkeeper and rooming house owner on St. Louis Avenue, was one of these men. If any two men had a dispute in the Bottoms, they went to Fleming for a ruling and considered his decision final. Garrett Fleming died in 1890.

Emil Ruff was dubbed the "Bread King." His bakery at Ninth and Hickory Streets kept the Bottoms well supplied with bread and pastries. When Emil died in 1900, he left an estate of $50,000.00. One personage of the early Bottoms era was James (Alderman) Pendergast, whose democratic organization was later shaped by his younger brother, Tom, into the Pendergast dynasty of the 1930's.

The Bottoms was a quiet village south of Twelfth Street made up of hard working, amiable people. They played as hard as they toiled frequenting the good time joints and gin mills on Union Avenue, St. Louis Avenue and Ninth Streets.

The isolation began to dissipate after the Union Depot opened in the Bottoms in 1878. The area became even closer to the city on the bluffs when the Twelfth Street and Ninth Street cable cars were built in 1885 and 1887. Travelers waiting for trains wandered in and out of the saloons and gambling houses located on Union Avenue near the old depot.

One of the most famous stretches in the Bottoms was known as the "Wet Block" extending east on Ninth Street from State Line. It boasted more saloons than any other "block" in the world, with twenty-four buildings and twenty-three saloons. This presented an often-raw image of Kansas

Figure 2 — Flood in West Bottoms, ca. 1894
Photo: Kansas City Library Photographs

City as a symbol of "The West."

Within a ten-year period, the Bottoms suffered many hardships. The great flood of 1903 sent water into the second story of many buildings. An even more devastating flood filled the Bottoms on July 13, 1951.

The Bottoms received a dramatic economic blow in 1914 when the new Union Station opened at Pershing and Main Streets. Union Station virtually wiped out business in the joints and saloons around the old depot on Union Avenue.

In 1918, the greatest fire in the city's history raged through the district. The fire started in the early evening on St. Louis Avenue and Santa Fe Street. Within an hour, a three-block radius was in flames. Wind carried sparks, igniting secondary fires in the stockyards and across the state line into Kansas. The fire damaged or destroyed forty businesses in the area. Losses were estimated at three million dollars, and the cause of the fire was never determined.

JOE WALKER

THE OFFICE of Jackson County Sheriff was created in 1828, and the first man to hold the office was forgotten long ago by the people of Jackson County. His many other accomplishments secure his legendary place in the history of the West. Joseph Reddeford Walker, known as trapper, guide, sheriff and horse thief, arrived in Independence, Missouri in 1819. He migrated from Virginia by way of Tennessee. In 1819, he joined Colonel Stephen Cooper. They ventured to Taos to establish trade and secure horses, but were forced out by the Spanish regime and returned to Independence, Missouri.

Joe Walker trapped and traded in that area for several years. Then in 1825, the government decided to finance a survey to determine the best route to Santa Fe, New Mexico. He appropriated $10,000.00 to cover expenses and $20,000.00 to barter with the Indians. The government chose General George Sibley of Fort Osage to organize the expedition. Walker was a natural for this venture because of his experience in the Taos territory. They selected Bill Williams, an infamous western entity, to act as the interpreter.

The expedition stopped about one hundred and forty-two miles southwest of their departure point. This allowed Williams to council with the Osage Indians to secure rights of passage and permission to hunt food in safety on the Indian Territory. The site where Williams halted the expedition retains the name of "Council Grove."

The Indian tribes holding land on this trail were the Osage and the (Kausies) Kansans, and Bill Williams was amiable with both. This made it a simple matter to obtain permission to set up markers for others using this route. Walker affixed his name to the treaty, and he returned to Independence to serve one term as Sheriff. Later he joined a party of seasoned mountain men, led by Silvester Cerre of St. Louis, Missouri. The group headed into Wyoming's Green River area on an expedition of trading and exploring. While attending the mountain men's July rendezvous, Walker met Captain Benjamin Bonneville whose name is associated with the Salt Flats of Utah. Captain Bonneville was eager for any knowledge of the California Country. He organized a party of fifty men, headed by Joe Walker, to make the initial crossing over the Sierra Nevada Mountains into unexplored California. Zenas Leonard, Joe Meek, Bill Williams, William

Figure 3 — Joseph Reddeford Walker
Portrait by Alfred Jacob Miller (1837)
Photo Courtesy the Porter Collection, Hugh Chase Private Library

Godey and other mountain men accompanied Walker. They were all eager to make the journey because they had heard tales of beautiful senoritas, select wines, blooded horses, and tender beef. The chief attraction for these veteran mountain men was the challenge of unknown territory.

Walker and his men traveled from Green River to the Great Salt Lake, then along the Humboldt River to a lake that would later be named Walker Lake. From there they began to climb over the Sierra Nevada Mountains. This feat turned out to be difficult and perilous. Many of the party lost their lives attempting these difficult passages. Walker was mild in both spirit and manner. This meek manner nearly caused the failure of the expedition when the men became careless with their camp routines, supplies and equipment.

In 1845, Captain John C. Fremont's survey party made the first recorded crossing. Kit Carson and Joe Walker were the scouts. Joe Walker recorded the crossing and warned immigrants not to attempt the untried route. However, in 1846 twenty-three year old Lanford Hastings retraced Fremont's trail across the plains. Hastings convinced several immigrant parties to follow him. The Donner-Reed party, seeking a shortcut to California in 1846, attempted the "Hastings Cutoff" in spite of Walker's warnings. They failed to take enough water and lost a critical number of oxen. They abandoned four of their wagons ten miles northeast of the Salt Flats. The delay resulted in their late arrival to the Sierra Nevada Mountains and a tragic winter.

At times, the men were in danger of starvation, while nearby Digger Indians shrewdly feasted on the horses and dogs that strayed from the main party. The Diggers were very primitive. Their normal diet consisted of bugs, grasshoppers, and roots from desert plants. They trailed the party like shadows, taking their animals and stealing traps that the men depended upon to secure their food. They grew so bold in their thievery that Walker's men found it necessary to kill fifty of them. Necessity drove them to eat their own mounts before the twenty-one day struggle across the mountains ended.

When they arrived at what is now known as Yosemite, all their troubles faded. Magnificent giant redwood trees surrounded them with scenery so beautiful they were mesmerized. The expedition forged on to the San Joaquin Valley, passing San Francisco and winding up their journey at Monterrey. However, the party gained little, if any, desired information. This failure was because of the attitude of the men taking part. While guests of the San Fernando Rye Mission, their behavior was so crude, they were asked to leave. In January, they returned to Monterrey to visit the Spanish Governor. He offered Walker a large parcel of land in an ambitious attempt to influence and encourage Walker to bring carpenters and other skilled tradesmen to the area. Walker turned down the offer, knowing his men were anxious to return to the life they knew best—mountains and wilderness. In February of 1834, he again started across the Sierras with three hundred head of blooded Spanish horses that he "neglected" to pay for. On their return trip, they crossed the mountains more to the south by a pass, which bore Walker's name from that day on. The cattle and horses began to die and as they died, the men sustained their own lives drinking the blood and eating the flesh of the expiring livestock.

In early summer, the exhausted party reached the Great Salt Basin. They lost no time in joining Bonneville near Bear Lake. When Walker informed Bonneville about their episodes of killing the Diggers and being involved in other crude and criminal activities while in California, Bonneville became furiously indignant and considered the expedition an utter failure. Today, that expedition is regarded as a major feat in Western history. However, others at Fort Bonneville rendezvous were elated with news of California and pledged they would make the trip.

Figure 4 — Illustration of Frontier
Hugh Chase Private Library

In 1839, Walker attended another meeting at Fort Bonneville, located at the junction of Horse Creek and Green River. Here he encountered Major Andrew Dripps, who had settled his family in what became known as Mulkey Square in Kansas City.

Walker made another trip to Los Angeles in 1841. On this trip, he carried out another horse raid with even more lucrative success. He had learned his lessons well from the previous calamity. He returned to Missouri with an excellent herd of Spanish steeds in tip-top condition.

In the fall of 1843, Walker joined Joseph B. Chiles, who was head of a wagon train of immigrants, at Fort Bridger, Wyoming. The train split and Walker led one section of the wagon train to California by way of Walker's Pass. He returned with another herd of horses, overtaking John Fremont on his third expedition at Las Vegas. He accompanied this expedition to Bents Fort. Captain John Fremont chose Walker as guide on his third expedition into California territory. This expedition traveled down the Humboldt Plays. They achieved the crossing of the Sierras with great difficulty. Walker returned to the Rocky Mountains just before Mexico's revolt from Spain.

In April of 1847, Walker was again living in Jackson County. He stayed in Jackson County for nearly two years. Walker was one of the first to take part in the gold rush of 1849. He grew wealthy, not mining for gold, but selling cattle to the miners. He did some successful prospecting later in the area of Prescott, Arizona. Walker eventually gave up the nomadic life and settled in Contra Casta, California. He remained there until his death in the fall of 1876.

BIRTH OF A CITY

ONE-EYED ELLIS was not wealthy; he was never accused of being a hero. He never appeared ambitious, yet he played an important part in the conception of a city. One-eyed Ellis was a man known as one who preferred to conduct business the easy way. He would sit in the door of his log cabin and wait for the customer to come to him.

Were he alive today, One-eyed Ellis would surely be dubbed "the town character." Ellis had his way of knowing the comings and goings of almost everyone in the young frontier community. One would believe his knowledge of events came about from his spending so much time in his doorway waiting for his customers. One-eyed Ellis knew much about

Figure 5 — Sketch by Officer Bill Cronley
The Informant — February 1970

John C. McCoy, a principal in the founding of Kansas City. What Ellis missed by having only one eye, he easily picked up with his super-sensitive hearing.

There was no doubt that Ellis knew very well why Bill Sublett attended the auction of the deceased Gabriel Prudhomme's property. He was there to represent the newly organized "Kansas Town Company." Any doubts as to why the fourteen gentlemen wished to acquire the property soon became evident.

It was a cold day in November 1838. A whistling wind, biting deep, came down the Missouri River as a small group interested in the auction huddled together on the levee. The auction began. When the bidding ended, Captain Bill Sublett, authorized representative for the Kansas Town Company, made the highest bid and bought 271 acres of rugged land. The chilling wind coming in off the river forced all of the fourteen-member company to seek warmth upon completion of the sale. They found this in the hickory wood burning fireplace in the cabin of One-eyed Ellis. The effect of this move was like freezing One-eyed Ellis and his cabin into a permanent place in the history of Kansas City.

After the group grew warm and a bit more comfortable, the first business meeting convened. The business associates felt that the first order of business should be the election of a chairman. It was decided this chairman should be one that understood the law. Since Ellis served as Justice of the Peace, one member suggested he would be just the right man. This caught Ellis completely by surprise, and left him somewhat flustered. He nodded his head in a gesture of disbelief. After some serious discussion, One-eyed Ellis, a man without ambition and less wealth or position, was elected chairman of the first meeting held by the founders of Kansas City.

By a twist of fate, Ellis sat in the company of fourteen leading citizens to conduct this important meeting held by the Town of Kansas Company. They were setting down rules and protocol from the lost memory of his scanty legal train-

Figure 6 — Post Card of old City Market and Red Brick City Hall
Published by Paul Eskensay of Kansas City, 1910
Photo: Kansas City Library Special Collections

ing. It was his responsibility to conduct this meeting. The main order of business was to select the name for the town.

Ellis taxed his mind. He was attempting to recall, to bring out the legal procedure from his poor talent and meager training. This responsibility was vastly different from his duties of affixing a signature to a document. The fire blazed flickering shadows on the wall, while One-eyed Ellis sat as the chairman at the meeting where men were in earnest discussion for a suitable name for their newly acquired town. Ellis usually lived his life from day-to-day in a gloomy cabin. For a short span of time, he became an important member of the new community that was to grow and become a great metropolis. One of the founders commented, "This was his only claim to being a celebrity, except he was known to sell remarkably bad whiskey to the Indians." Ellis was never asked again to preside over a meeting and that was the last ever held by that group of men.

Figure 7 — Sketch by Officer Bill Cronley
The Informant – February 1970

Future meetings meant little to Ellis. The one meeting they held in his humble cabin under the bluff near the levee in 1838 helped secure his place in history. It was he, One-eyed Ellis, elected chairman of the group. It was he, One-eyed Ellis, who stood with the distinguished men as they rose to their feet and declared, "Gentlemen, we shall name our City 'The Town of Kansas'."

KANSAS CITY

OVER ONE HUNDRED AND FORTY-NINE YEARS AGO, the Jackson County Court issued the order establishing the "Town of Kansas." This "Town of Kansas" became known as Kansas City, Missouri. Three plots of land made up of bluffs and gulleys along the Missouri River were incorporated. This area, made up of 256 acres, was purchased for $4,220.00 from the estate of Gabriel Prudhomme.

The gentlemen responsible for making that purchase were fourteen men who would become the original incorporators of our city in 1850. They were William L. Sublette, Moses G. Wilson, Oliver C. Caldwell, Fry P. McGee, John C. McCoy, William Miles Chick, Abraham Fonda, George W. Tate, Samuel C. Owens, Russell Hicks, Jacob Ragan, William Collins, James Stewart and John Campbell.

At this time, the state of Kansas was nonexistent. The

Figure 8 — Kansas City, 1855
Photo: Hugh Chase Private Library

town was named after the Kansas River, often referred to as the Kaw. This name was naturally adopted because the Kanza (Kawsa) Indians lived in the area. Many names were suggested such as Kawsmouth, Possum Hallow, just to name a few. Many of the settlers began calling it the town of Kansas. The name seemed to have caught on and had received the approval of the men who acted to incorporate it in 1839. In 1850, they made it official.

Missouri gained acceptance into the Union as a state in 1821. The organization of Jackson County took place in 1826. The Santa Fe Trail had its start and the settlement began to grow. The first post office opened on May 3, 1847, in a store owned by Mr. Chick on the bank of the Missouri River. Stagecoach and steamboat received and dispatched the mail.

The year of 1850 is the first date that legally and officially affects the city. Two other dates shown in history are also legal and official. In a special act of the Missouri legislature in February 1853, the Town of Kansas became the "City of Kansas." In March 1853, that same year, the voting

Figure 9 — William Miles Chick (left) and John C. McCoy (right)
Photos: K.C. Library — Special Collections

population (consisting of thirty men), went to the polls to ratify the act of legislature. The organization of the Kansas Territory was not until 1854, long after the name had been selected as a town site in Missouri. This acts as proof that Kansas City was named before, and not after, the State of Kansas.

William Rockhill Nelson, newspaperman and founder of the *Kansas City Star,* thought the name was confusing and made a strong attempt to change the name to Westport. His idea and effort nearly caused a riot. He abandoned the idea and admitted defeat after finding how much the citizens were against the idea.

The son of Daniel Boone, famous pioneer and scout Daniel Morgan Boone, is thought to be the first to see and explore the site where Kansas City is now located. He was so pleased with the area surrounding it as a place to trap, fish, and hunt that he chose this area to live out the rest of his life. His final resting place is a site near Sixty-Third Street and The Paseo.

A few years after Daniel Morgan Boone had explored the area, Lewis and Clark visited this site on their famous historical expedition. Chouteau and his French trappers were the next people to show interest in the area. They located a trading post for the American Fur Company at the foot of the bluffs, which is now known as Cliff Drive. The floods in 1826 caused so much damage to their buildings that it forced them to move farther up the river where the city actually had its beginning.

The estate of Gabriel Prudhomme took in an area of approximately sixty square blocks. Kansas City now covers an area of between three hundred sixteen and three hundred seventeen square miles.

UNION CEMETERY

ANYONE WITH MORE than a passing interest in area history will find a visit to Union Cemetery more than a rewarding experience. At first, one is very surprised when entering the gates. You feel that you have just left the hustle and bustle of a busy city and stepped back into a spot of shaded tranquility. Beautiful, well-manicured grounds surround and envelope you in quiet and peace.

After becoming acquainted with the surroundings one starts to notice some of the names on the silent shrines and monuments — some very famous, some unknown. You find yourself wishing the ghosts and spirits could come to life and relate early day occurrences only they might know about Kansas City. It would be exciting to question each one on their part in building the vast area into what we know and see today.

Jacob Ragan's resting place is marked by a tall monument at the south end of the cemetery. He was one of the early city fathers. He served with Admiral Perry at Lake Erie. John Calvin McCoy, founder of Westport, rests not far from Mr. Ragan. He was another early father of Kansas City. His wife, Victoria Chick McCoy, died during the cholera epidemic of 1849. Dr. Johnston Lykins, Kansas City's first actual mayor, is also buried in this area along with Thomas A. Smart, an early owner of most of the downtown property. Allen B. H. McGee, leader in the city of Westport and one of the original purchasers of the Prudhomme Estate, also lies in this area. The list of greats seems never-ending.

Various authors have written many books about the outstanding feats of Alexander Majors. He was best known for his freighting business throughout the southwest. Majors, along with Russell and Waddell, is also credited with the founding of the "Pony Express." He was the one who convinced the U. S. Government to unload cargo from the riverboats at the bend in the river instead of traveling on north to Leavenworth, Kansas. This was one of his biggest contributions toward the early economy.

George Caleb Bingham was an artist of great fame who returned to make his home in Kansas City. The Missouri Legislature appointed him to the Board of Police Commissioners. He served that board and the citizens of Kansas City well as the second president of that body. One of Bingham's greatest claims to historical fame was his painting of "General Order Number 11." It is generally thought that he stopped the nomination of General Ewing as a can-

Figure 10 - Monument to 15 Confederate Soldiers
Photo: Kansas City Library Images of Kansas City

didate for the office of President of the United States using this famous painting as a weapon.

W.W. Payne was in the ice business. His residence was on Reservoir Hill. His brother, Milton J. Payne, was one of the founders of the cemetery. He served six elected terms as mayor of Kansas City. His first term was in 1855.

Joseph Boggs purchased a farm at Nineteenth and Vine. His claim to fame was serving as a lieutenant in the American Revolution. He died in 1843. He was first interred in the Yoacham Cemetery in Westport and later moved to Union Cemetery.

Jesse Riddlesbarger was the owner of the second established newspaper in Kansas City, "The Enterprise." He sold the paper to Robert T. Van Horn. He remained active in Kansas City business circles until the enforcement of Order Number 11. After that, he suffered bankruptcy. He then left for St. Louis, Missouri.

Many bodies were moved to Union Cemetery from a graveyard at Missouri Avenue and Oak. Among the bodies moved from that location was that of William M. Chick. He was the first postmaster and an early merchant in Kansas City. He deserves credit for getting much of the Santa Fe trade for Kansas City. Independence and Westport dominated that trade before then.

There is a small block over the grave of Charles E. Kearney. He was a successful and leading businessman in both Kansas City and Westport. He was president of the Cameron and Kansas City Railroad. He played a very active part in the Hannibal Bridge being built across the Missouri River at Kansas City.

One of the headstones tells a tragedy of the past. In 1866, a young man rode out with his brother, a deputy marshal. They pursued several men who had robbed a wagon train at Shawnee Mission, Kansas. They overtook and confronted the robbers on the banks of the Blue River. A shoot-out followed and a seventeen-year-old youngster died. For several years

Figure 11 - Two Crypts in Union Cemetery
Photo: Kansas City Library Images of Kansas City

thereafter any person who was passing Forty-first and Agnes could see a headstone with the word "MURDERED" inscribed on it.

John Campbell donated the city's first fire engine. He was also a leader in Kansas City activities. One of our streets bears Campbell's name. The street named after his wife, Charlotte, is a short distance away. This street runs south through the city. His home, a large mansion, was located at the southeast corner of Second and Campbell. In later years, his mansion was converted into a hospital.

Josephine Anderson, a nineteen-year-old lady, was accused of being a Southern sympathizer. She was imprisoned in a building at 1409 Grand Avenue with several other young ladies. She died when the building collapsed. Her brother was so embittered over her death that he took up the life of a guerrilla soldier. He backed the rebel cause with violence and was soon known as "Bloody Bill Anderson."

Another well-known city founder interred in the Union

Cemetery is William Gillis. He was the first man to own and operate a hotel in Kansas City. His money was used to build the Gillis Theater. This theater helped to finance and maintain the Gillis Orphan Home.

Fifteen confederate soldiers, wounded and captured in the Battle of Westport, received treatment in any structure that could be used as a hospital. Doctor Isaac M. Ridge and Doctor Caleb Winfrey treated them. The prisoners succumbed to their injuries in spite of the work to save them. Edward Stine received and prepared the bodies for burial. The sexton of Union Cemetery then received and buried them in a plot belonging to John P. Withers. A wooden stake marked each grave. Families of three of these soldiers later claimed the bodies and took them to central Missouri for reburial. Twelve bodies remain resting near a tall memorial erected years ago.

These are just a few of the names that can be recognized and incidents recalled from the past involving the men and women resting here. There are as many stories about these people as there are monuments in these peaceful surroundings.

ORGANIZATION

IN AMERICA, between the years of 1845 and 1855, city councils largely controlled police departments and administrative responsibilities lodged with the common council. The office of mayor held little broad executive power at this time. The modern police system began unfolding on the eastern seaboard. About this time the first monthly mail coach between Independence, Missouri and Santa Fe, New Mexico started and Kansas City was incorporated as the "Town of Kansas." This land is now bounded by the Missouri River, Broadway, Forest Avenue, and the section line that now crosses Main Street at Missouri Avenue. In 1851, the first state aid was granted to build railroads. The first railroad established in Missouri was the Pacific Railroad in St. Louis. In 1851, the first newspaper began operation in the Town of Kansas. Then in 1853, the name changed to the "City of Kansas." The State granted the original formal charter on February 22, 1889. Seven extensive statutes were made in this period.

Between the period of 1856 and 1858, the Board of Trade was being organized. During 1858, the first telegraph operated in the city. At that time, the east had state controlled police bodies. These set examples in creating an administrative body called the "Board of Police Commissioners," consisting of the Mayor, Recorder and City Judge. This set a general pattern, which many communities copied with modifications. Missouri maintained a strong centralized control over its police forces due to its location as a border state during the Civil

War. Kansas City's Board of Police Commissioners, under state law, was instituted in 1861. This act provided the City of Kansas with a Board of Police Commissioners that consisted of three members and the Mayor. Members had to be citizens of the State of Missouri for one year prior to appointment. The Police Commissioners could hold their office for only one year and received twenty-five dollars per annum as salary, payable quarterly. The Mayor and commissioners were required to take an oath to support the constitution of Missouri. The majority of the board would constitute a quorum. The commissioners were to appoint a competent police force of no more than twenty-five members. The police manpower might be increased in extraordinary occasions. The officers of police were to consist of one captain, two lieutenants, and one turnkey, with officers not to exceed fifteen. Their pay was ten dollars a week, payable monthly. The Board estimated annually the sum of money necessary to discharge their duties. They also requested the council to make appropriations of sums out of the general revenue after paying interest debts owed by the city. The Board swore to bring all persons arrested before the recorder of the City of Kansas (or some justice of the peace) to be dealt with according to law. The common council could pass ordinances, though no ordinance would conflict with the powers of the Board of Police Commissioners or hinder them in the discharge of their sworn duties.

During 1868 to 1870, it is rumored that Wyatt Earp learned gun fighting from Kansas City's Chief of Police Thomas Speers and his cronies. In 1884, the Kansas City Court of Appeal was established. The first show-up (line-up) came into existence, along with photos of criminals. By 1870, Chief Speers could boast of having over 1,000 photographs in his rogue's gallery. One picture played a very important part in the identification of the James Gang. In 1872, Chief Speers required that men rack their guns before coming into the city. Many flags flew at half-mast upon the death of Chief Thomas M. Speers in 1896.

MAJORS HOUSE

SAM WALTER FOSS might have had in mind the house at 8145 State Line and the man who built it when he penned these lines: "Let me live in my house by the side of the road and be a friend of man." Both the house and the man have more than proved their friendship for mankind. Both made a worthy contribution to the generations of men over the past century. Alexander Majors, the man who built and lived in this house, was senior partner in the freighting firm of Russell, Majors and Waddell. This firm organized and operated the Pony Express from St. Joseph, Missouri to Sacramento, California in 1860 and 1861.

Alexander Majors started out a very colorful and exciting career as a farmer in Cass County. He later turned freighter. In 1848, Alexander Majors purchased six wagons and enough oxen to draw them. He wrote a pledge and required his bullwhackers to sign before he would accept them in his employ. This pledge spoke plainly in stating that any man accepted would not swear, mistreat the animals or drink hard liquor. He would tolerate only sober, God-fearing employees.

Equipped in this manner, he contracted to haul cargo from Independence or Westport to Santa Fe, New Mexico. He departed on his first trip August 10, 1848 and returned November 3, 1848. He made the round trip in the record time of ninety-two days. In 1849, he made another trip. In 1850, the business required ten wagons and one hundred thirty oxen. His earnings for that year were $13,000. Before the year was out, he had a contract to transport more than fifty tons of military supplies from Fort Leavenworth to Fort McKay near what is now Dodge City, Kansas.

Majors' business grew to the point in 1854 that he needed one hundred wagons and twelve-hundred oxen to transport cargo. Russell, a merchant and dreamer, observed and made plans. They formed a partnership in the spring of 1855. On March 27, 1855, a contract signed under the name of Majors and Russell granted them a monopoly to transport all military supplies west of the Missouri River. In a short while, they owned many businesses boasting the name of Russell, Majors and Waddell.

It was significant that the expansion of Russell, Majors and Waddell's business and Kansas City's phenomenal increase in population were simultaneous. The increase of the firm's freighting business was one of the major factors in giving Kansas City its initial impetus toward greatness.

Prior to 1851, government supplies for forts to the west were unloaded at Wayne City, north of Independence. When Alexander Majors began contracting for the transportation

Figure 12 - "Le Poney-Post"
Early French Artist Concept of Pony Express
Hugh Chase Private Library

of these goods, he set out to induce the government to unload the steamboats at Westport Landing. At that time rivalry between the river towns of Weston, Atchison, Leavenworth, and Wayne City was at a peak. Whichever city became the unloading point would hold a great advantage over the others.

He was unable to accomplish this until 1857. In that year, Majors received influential assistance from men in Washington. He then persuaded John B. Lloyd, Secretary of War, to issue the coveted order in favor of Kansas City. Wayne City died and the growth of other river towns declined because of this order. Meanwhile, Kansas City enjoyed an unprecedented period of growth. Alexander Majors had more to do with laying the foundation for that early period of prosperity from 1855 to 1859 than any other person.

In the spring of 1858, Russell, Majors and Waddell received a huge government contract to transport sixteen million pounds of freight to Utah for General A. S. Johnston's army of 25,000 men. They also contracted to carry five million pounds from Fort Leavenworth or Fort Riley, Kansas to Fort Union in New Mexico. Their business for that year was so great that they held what amounted to a monopoly of the government freighting business across the plains. In his book *Seventy Years on the Frontier*, Mr. Majors stated, "We had to increase from three to four hundred wagons and teams we previously owned to 3,500 wagons and teams, and it required more than 40,000 oxen to draw the supplies. We also used a thousand mules and employed 4,000 men."

When Russell, Majors and Waddell moved their headquarters to Kansas City, other big freighters such as Irwins, Jackmans and Parkers soon followed. Kansas City quickly became the busiest place on the river—the chief point of departure for all regions of the west. The levee was crowded with white covered wagons harnessed to the most diminutive mules. The rough and hideous looks of the accompanying skinners made ladies shudder.

Figure 13 - Early Photo of Majors House
Hugh Chase Private Library

The coming of Russell, Majors and Waddell quickened every phase of youthful Kansas City. Warehouses for storage of goods, homes for employees, and stores of every kind were built. Banks boasted capital amounting to as much as $2,241,217. They reported sales of 16,000 horses, mules and oxen, 864,000 stock cattle, 5,063 hogs and 1,825 sheep. During this period, Russell, Majors and Waddell bought 70,000 work cattle in one year.

The Majors house was completed in 1856. The 320-acre farm chosen for the home site was acquired from the government in the 1840's. Following the formation of the partnership on December 28, 1845, the farm became a pasture for oxen.

This interesting old house originally contained nine very large rooms with high ceilings. It was a splendid specimen of American architecture. The doors and the casings, as well as the ornamental moldings, are of virgin pine, a material that no longer exists. The original floors were of broad tongue and groove pine.

Four years after the building was completed, the Civil War started. The Majors' farm was a favorite camping place for both Union and Confederate troops. On at least one occasion, the notorious guerilla leader Charles Quantrell spent several days with his followers. One of the main reasons it was popular as a campsite was that a famous spring, which gushed gallons of cool water, was located here. This spring never dried up. When order #11 was enacted, the family living there was vacated from the house, but nothing was disturbed because it belonged to Alexander Majors, the great government freighter.

Following the Civil War the ownership changed to the Poteet family. In 1900, Mr. A. Louis Ruhl purchased it for use as his country home. When his children left home, he moved to Kansas City and divided the farm into what is

Figure 14 - Later Photo of Majors House
Hugh Chase Private Library

known as Crest Arche Hills. He converted the old Majors' farm into a school and community building to interest families with children to locate in the neighborhood. For years following, it functioned as the "Community House" for that district.

After some years, a school district was established in the addition and a new modern school building was proposed. At first, the plans put the new building on the site of the old house, and a contract was let to raze the house. The workmen appeared on the scene to start their work. After working one day, the contractor reported that it was almost impossible to wreck the building due to the massive construction with square hand-cut nails and crossbeams. They made other plans and selected a different site. Majors' house was offered for sale.

Miss Louise P. Johnston, a teacher at East High School,

Figure 15 - Youthful Alexander Majors (left) and Mature Alexander Majors (right)
Hugh Chase Private Library

purchased the house. She had a familial interest in the old house. Her maternal grandmother was Missouri Majors, the daughter of Alexander Majors. Missouri Majors married R. Duke Simpson in 1860. Mrs. Johnson purchased the house in 1932, but she didn't occupy the house until 1939. She made the old mansion her permanent home until her death. She carried a dream of an extensive restoration and reconstruction to the grave.

The house, like the gentleman who built it, stands as a shrine to the opening and development of the early west. Several years ago, the home was remodeled and restored to what it was when Majors pictured it as his dream home. It stands as a living monument to the firm of Russell, Majors and Waddell, the three men who saw nothing as impossible in their time.

CITY GROWTH

MANY GALLONS OF WATER have flowed down the Missouri River since the rough buildings and wind-blown houses sparsely lining the levee became “The Town of Kansas” and attained the dignity of a formally organized community. Booms boosting trade came and the town spread, like arms reaching out, in search of growth. Winding roads from every direction made their way down to the small village on the levee. Early day bigwigs built awe-inspiring mansions atop Quality Hill. Newer neighborhoods became fashionable, leading to their desertion. Fortunately, because of location, the trading posts and river landing grew into a booming metropolis for the rich farming and cattle lands stretched between Kansas City and the Rocky Mountains.

As the years passed, business and the rest of the city grew away from the banks of the river. In the 1850’s, the heart of the town was the public square, bounded by Main and Walnut Streets. Here, farmers from the surrounding areas brought their fresh produce to market. Trappers trod through the dust and mud of the square to exchange tales of their long lonely months on the plains. The saloons roared as men who spent lonely months following uncivilized trails returned to “civilization.”

For much of the population at that time this square became the hub of the rapidly growing city. Inexorably, the town continued to move south. The city government stubbornly stuck to the square, and for many years its official seat of government was in the succession of city halls erected on the west side of the square. Now even that small hold to the turbulent past has been broken. The old City Hall has given way to a modern white tower structure located nearer the business life of the city.

The public square had been the seat of city government since construction of the first City Hall in 1857. At that time, the southern city limits were at Ninth Street. The site of the present City Hall at Eleventh and Oak Streets was uncleared timberland outside of town. The first plat of the Town of Kansas, which was without municipal government, was filed in 1889. It embraced the land running from the river south to Second Street and from Elm Street just west of Delaware, known today as Grand Avenue.

The second plat enlarged the village limits. This second plat provided a town square at the edge of town and all businesses were located on the levee along the riverfront. The

Figure 16 - First City Hall, Built in 1857
Photo: Hugh Chase Private Library

new boundaries were the river, Independence Avenue, Central Street, and Oak Street.

The town officially became "The City of Kansas" or "Kansas City," February 22, 1853, when the state legislature granted a charter. The first City Council met April 15, 1853, a few days following the first election. During the first five years of the community's history as a city, the seat of the municipal government was the second floor of various business buildings along the levee. One of the buildings, according to legend, was a saloon.

First mention of the location of the city offices appears in the early records of the minutes of the city council meeting of November 4, 1854. The Council allowed the claim of G. Benelein the sum of $12, four month's rent of a council room at the rate of three dollars a month. On April 15, 1855, the Council recognized the need for larger quarters and rented a room from Al Gilhan for $25 effective until January 1, 1856. Meanwhile, the Council considered requests for permanent quarters on December 10, 1855.

At that meeting on December 10, 1885, the Council authorized Mayor A.J. Payne to proclaim an election of real estate owners to borrow money for the construction of a "Town Hall." Two months later, records show a report from the mayor that the proposal had gone down to defeat. The City Officials, believing that the community of three hundred was destined for greatness, weren't shocked by the results of the election. They proceeded with an alternate plan for improvements, including a City Hall.

Tax collections were very good in 1856; so on October 13 of that year, the Council enacted an ordinance authorizing construction of a City Hall and market place on the public square. For many years, this site housed the City Hall and the city officials, and the current revenues paid the cost.

On November 3, 1856, less than a month later, the Council confirmed a contract for construction of a City Hall with J. W. Ammons. Mr. Ammons was elected a member of the Council one year later. The contract price was $3,570 for the building (less the roof). Another contractor constructed the roof.

The site of Kansas City's first City Hall was the northwest corner of the city square, Fourth and Main Streets. Construction started in 1857 and the building was completed the next year, while M. J. Payne was serving his second term as Mayor. This model City Hall, constructed of brick, made the citizenry proud.

This structure combined city market and City Hall. The ground on which it sat was so damp and unstable that the hall had to be constructed on piling. This gave it the appearance of being on stilts. Brick later encased the piling and greatly improved the appearance. The greater part of the first floor contained a market house. City offices arched over the remaining part of the first floor. The second floor contained a hall used for public meetings, dances, and other social affairs. At that time, the Catholics and Methodists were the only religious bodies with church buildings in the city, so all other Christian denominations held their meetings in the town hall.

Kansas City was already a trading center, which moved five million dollars worth of merchandise each year in the Santa Fe trade alone, before construction of the first City Hall. Businessmen asked the State Legislature that a court of common pleas with jurisdiction in criminal and civil cases in the Kaw Township convene here. The upstairs hall of the city building held this court and the market downstairs became city offices for the first City Marshal, John F. Hayden, and the clerk of the newly established court. They accomplished this by bricking up the space between the arches of the market. A wooden market house was built east of the City Hall on the site of the current city market.

For a time after creation of the Court of Common Pleas, the Mayor and City Council held their meetings at 410 Main Street across from the City Hall. This arrangement continued until the legislature established the Circuit Courts there.

This abolished the court of common pleas. They then built a new courthouse. The Mayor, the City Council and other officials who were crowded out, returned to quarters in the City Hall. Municipal Court convened on the first floor and the second floor became a place for charity gatherings and other social functions.

For thirty years, the first city hall was the focal point of Kansas City. Thomas (Tom) M. Speers came to that building as City Marshal in 1870. He is considered by many historians to be the most famous and efficient peace officer this city ever had. Tom Speers served Kansas City for more than thirty-four years, first as City Marshal in the first City Hall. After that, he served as Chief of Police in the next City Hall. He worked as a freighter on the plains and as an officer in the San Francisco Vigilantes during the gold rush in 1849 and 1850. For almost a quarter of a century, the citizens of Kansas City knew him as Chief of Police. Those who ignored or flaunted the law knew him as a terror.

As the city grew, the City Hall became too small for the enlarged departments of the city government, and most of them were crowded out. The Mayor and the City Council went to the Nelson Building. The Board of Public Works went to the Lockridge Building. Other city offices operated out of the Exchange Building. The City Hall was completely given over to the Police Department and was soon known as "Police Headquarters." There were many who talked about the need for a new City Hall for years. There was considerable opposition to such a project because of the cost involved. Finally, all opposition gave way to the Kansas City spirit of progress in May 1889, when bonds were voted and issued for public improvement. This opened the doors for planning the construction of a new City Hall.

MENSING ISLAND

VERY FEW KANSAS CITIANS know that the very spot where the Kansas City Power and Light Company's station in the East Bottoms stands was once an island. This island was a successful Trading Post for Francis and Cyprien Chouteau. It was a military base during the War Between the States. John H. Mensing, a German immigrant, settled and occupied this island. John Mensing farmed the land while fighting off Indians and many squatters. He went to court over the question of title, but he died without winning the fight. His children carried on this battle without success.

The island, now a part of the mainland, was first Chouteau Island and then Grandstaff Island. It was later Mensing's Island after John Mensing settled with his family around 1857. As then constituted, the island comprised about fifty-seven acres and later increased to an estimated one hundred thirty acres as the river caused accretion. This accretion was the start of Mensing's troubles.

John H. Mensing arrived in the United States in 1836. He first stopped in St. Louis and proceeded to Kansas City. He saw Kansas City as a raw settlement on the bluffs overlooking the muddy Missouri River. Mensing first took residence in a section centered on Third and Oak Streets. Henry Mensing, eldest of several children, was born there on March 1, 1857.

Mensing filed application for the government patent to the island, which extended from Prospect to Lydia Avenue, but the patent was never granted. The government designated the island as a military base. The army occupied it during the Civil War. Use of the island as an army post proved unsuccessful. The fickle Missouri River cut away the land under the structures as rapidly as they were erected.

The Mensing home, however, seemed immune to the vulgarities and rude treatment the river served most people. It remained undisturbed. The government gave up any idea of building a usable and satisfactory post. In 1864, they abandoned the island.

Then began the contest to acquire, by private interest, a title to the land the Mensing family held by virtue of possession. The shallow channel that separated the island from the mainland gradually filled with silt; the island became larger and the channel narrower. Mensing and others spent great sums of money in an attempt to gain title to the island. Judge Guinotte, owner of the Kansas City Land Com-

Figure 17 - Outskirts of Kansas City, ca. 1860's
Hugh Chase Private Library

pany, figured in this litigation. Judge Guinotte claimed his father had purchased this property from the Chouteau's but never took possession.

Grandstaff was a typical western pioneer. For many years he operated a sawmill on Pacific Street, east of Harrison. The sawmill demanded so much of his time that he too, abandoned the island. Several years later, Mensing occupied the island. He bought a tract of land from Joseph Guinotte on the mainland shore at the same time. He established a much-needed grocery store and sold food and other necessary items.

John H. Mensing died in 1897, still thwarted in his efforts to win title to the land. He left his children to carry on this unsuccessful fight.

COATES HOUSE

THE COATES HOUSE has seen its share of glorious moments, fame, fortune and tragedy. Its past is Kansas City's past; its future is Kansas City's future.

On January 22, 1978, a raging fire blazed fiercely in one of Kansas City's most enduring landmarks. The yellow, blue, and red fingers of flame that swept through the frigid air and snuffed out twenty lives dealt what many presumed to be a final blow to the Coates House.

History documents the house as the grand old dowager of downtown buildings. Her 1005 Broadway address assured her of a vital role in the activities and important decisions so essential to the growth of the city. For over a century, she housed her secrets, reveled in her moments of glory, and flirted with the great and near-great who signed her guest book. Moreover, like the lady she was, the Coates House accepted physical deterioration with a calm face befitting her character.

Construction of the Coates House began in 1860. When the Civil War started, the foundation was completed and one wall was erected as high as the first story. A shed stored and protected the workman's tools. The construction halted until after the war. Work on the building resumed in 1868, when Col. S. W. Eldridge sought financing by local interest, and T. S. Case, John R. Balis and Col. Kersey Coates raised the $20,000.00 necessary to finish the hotel.

The building was completed in 1869 and sold to Col.

Eldridge's brother, Major Thomas B. Eldridge, who opened it under the name of the Broadway Hotel. In 1872, Major Eldridge sold his interest to Col. Kersey Coates, who became the sole owner. The name changed after the transaction to the "Coates House."

One of the earlier guests to register at the hotel was Ulysses S. Grant. Grover Cleveland stayed at the Coates House on two occasions, once in 1868 during his first term in office as President. President Cleveland returned to the chic hotel on his honeymoon with his bride, Francis Folsen. She was the daughter of his former law partner. The newlyweds occupied Suite 215, which for years thereafter was known as the Cleveland Suite.

Richard P. Hobson, the gallant naval officer who sank the Merrimac in Santiago Harbor in 1898, visited the Coates House shortly after the close of the Spanish American War. Hobson's daring maritime maneuvers established him as a

Figure 18 - Coates House
Sketch: Hugh Chase Private Library

hero. More than forty women mobbed him as he registered, all of them seeking a glance of this valiant man. One lady managed to sneak a kiss from the dashing Admiral, and the other thirty-nine would not relent until he bestowed a similar greeting upon them. Thanks to this incident, Hobson became "Kissing Hobson," a nickname he carried to his grave.

In 1871, just prior to purchasing the hotel, Mr. Coates built an opera house just across the street. Because of its location and well-deserved reputation as the finest hotel west of the Mississippi, the Coates House generally attracted top theatrical stars. In the early days of American theater, stage celebrities toured alone and played their leading roles with the stock companies situated in all the larger cities. From those days, the hotel boasted such noted personalities as Maggie Mitchell, Josh Billings, Charlotte Cushman, Edwin Booth and the incomparable Fanny Brice.

The Coates House changed hands several times before 1929, but always remained meticulously maintained. On June 30, 1927, John A. McDonald, manager of the hotel's famous Turkish Bath since its opening in 1890, took a reporter on a tour of the pool. A victim of prohibition and the ensuing shortage of open-acknowledged hangovers, it was being closed for the final time. McDonald's eyes brimmed with tears as he recounted the bath's history. The following is a portion of the reporter's account on that tour:

"This morning the lions stare grimly into the blue waters of the marble swimming pool of the Coates House Turkish Bath. From their position on the pillars beside the pool, the beasts have stared into that water everyday for more than thirty-seven years, never blinking their eyes. This evening the stone eyes can rest. The pool was emptied for the last time. The bath, nationally famous and closely allied with Kansas City's history, will close." The shadows of days past walked with McDonald as he showed his visitor the elaborate rooms, the floors of highly polished Italian marble, the elegant furniture of a special manufacturer with coverings as plush

and as bright that day as they had been some thirty years before. The pool indeed, was beautiful, with its marble sides clearly visible below the water line, the gleaming brass shiny handrails leading down sculptured steps into the water. The reflection of the ornately fashioned overhead lights shimmered upon the water's glassy surface as McDonald regaled the reporter with fond remembrances of the great boxers who had used the spa as a gathering place between bouts. "Right here is where Bob Fitzsimmons was sitting when he visited Kansas City after his fight with Jim Corbett in Carson City, Nevada," McDonald said as he perched near the wall of the pool. "Bob was dressed in his evening clothes with big diamonds in his shirt studs and a top hat, and he was demonstrating the fight. His charade was a little more realistic than he intended, and he ended up in the pool—top hat and all! I was laughing so that after he climbed out, he picked me up and threw me in." McDonald pointed to a great iron ring that swooped out of the ceiling. "A punching bag used to hang from that," he explained, "and there were some real tunes played on it, too. Fitzsimmons used it. So did Jim Jeffries, Battling Nelson, Patty Partell and Jim Corbett."

The spotlight on the Coates House dimmed considerably after the pool closed. A restricted cash flow during the great depression and a concerted effort by Kansas City's financial leaders to develop other sections of the downtown area combined to reduce the aging hotel to step-sister status.

In the 1940's, the Coates House served her nation in time of war. Extensive remodeling made the house available for the overflow of service personnel, defense workers and their families who crowded into Kansas City, desperate for living quarters. Ninety of her great high ceiling rooms were converted into apartments, and one hundred and three other rooms were refurbished for use by temporary guests.

Her extensive facelift notwithstanding, abandonment of the Coates House occurred after the war for the more "modern" hotels erected to attract traveling salespeople, vacationers, and conventioneers. As the shadows of Kansas City's skyscrapers lengthened over her, the Coates House lovingly embraced a new Coates House. Her refugees huddled quietly at Tenth and Broadway until that arctic Sunday morning when screaming fire engines and probing cameras abruptly focused Kansas City's attention upon them.

The ashes were barely cool when speculation about the building's viability began. Various groups inspected her century of service as handmaiden of the community closely in an effort to determine her future. The Historic Kansas City Foundation realized that the sturdy structure supported by charred remnants of years of crude improvements should be saved, and they purchased the Coates House. Restoration of the Coates House is complete and she again entertains residents, while she patiently bides her time until a courtship with new generations of Kansas Citians begins.

TREASURE

IS A BURIED TREASURE HIDDEN, waiting to be discovered somewhere on Kansas City's west side? Will a construction worker find a wooden box rotted by time? Will he find inside this box thousands of dollars in twenty-dollar double eagles, gold and silver pieces tarnished by time, demand notes, and state script as dry as aged tobacco? Will hands shake and tremble as they remove the proud heirlooms of Kansas City's early families? They were valuable at that time but will carry a much higher value now because of their antiquity. Fate and time hold the answers to these questions. This much is known today …

On the night of October 21, 1864, just north of the Immaculate Conception Cathedral at 416 West Twelfth Street, a fortune was buried. As far as we know today, it was never found.

A trip back in time is necessary if we are to understand about the treasure. We must build a mental picture of Kansas City as it was over one hundred thirty-eight years ago on October 21, 1864. This could have been the darkest hour in the city's history.

First, we must take away the modern buildings. Replace them with the rustic brick and wooden structures of the 1860's era. The air is crisp and chilly. The scent of burning wood fills the fresh air as smoke curls upward from the chimneys. The fireplace is crackling and casting shadows with the first fires of fall.

This is the frontier in the midst of the Civil War. Half the population has fled, leaving two thousand inhabitants. The city limits ends on Troost Avenue on the east. The city stretches south to Twenty-Second Street. Beyond that, we see only fields and wooded hillsides, then the Town of Westport. Travel beyond this point may bring confrontations with Bushwhackers, Red Legs, and Jayhawkers. They are all there for diverse reasons, ready to pounce on the city should the opportunity present itself.

At the southwest corner of Tenth and Central Streets is Fort Union, the stronghold of Union Soldiers to guard the small city. A forty-pounder (cannon) mounted on a platform booms, calling the militia to arms. Between Tenth and Twelfth Streets on Broadway, the street rumbles with the sound of marching men, the clipped voices of command, and the rustle of shouldering rifles.

Construction of the Coates House halted because of the war. The soldiers used the boarded up foundation to stable their mounts. A line of breastwork began at Locust and Ninth Streets, near the site of the old Public Library. It crossed Main Street at Twelfth Street, and then ran near the bluff at Fourteenth and Main Streets. Now a frantic effort was underway

Figure 19 - Fort Union, 1861
Hugh Chase Private Library

to throw up a new fortification at Fourteenth and Oak Streets.

Commerce had slowed to a trickle because of the war. With one exception, all newspapers ceased publication. Guerrillas cut telegraph lines daily. Wagging tongues tell rumors of the public's action. Inflation sent the cost of a hundred pound bag of flour to seven dollars, if found. Interest rates soared to three per cent a month. People had faith in only two kinds of money ... silver and gold; they are hoarding both; waiting.

On this day, the people of Kansas City are very apprehensive. Two words sparked fear wherever men gather and talk ... "Price's raid." Even the dead and falling leaves appeared to whisper, "Price is coming," as they floated softly from the trees. General Sterling Price, victor of the Battle of Lexington, is making his way to Kansas City to attempt a daring dash for Fort Leavenworth.

In 1861, stories of Price's seizure of money from Lexington banks run rampant. Depositors filed into Kansas City banks to withdraw their money. They then faced the problem of its safekeeping. Would it be safe hidden in their homes when the confederate soldiers enter the city? They think not!

They turned to one man the entire community trusted, Father Bernard J. Donnelly, pastor of the Church of the Immaculate Conception. Father Donnelly had won the love and respect of the community eight years before. He brought some three hundred Irish immigrants into the city. With a Herculean effort, they were able to cut down the bluffs that had served to pinch the settlement so tightly against the riverbank. They opened the way to allow growth to the south.

Father Donnelly was born in County Cavan, Ireland. He was a stocky man with exceptionally wide shoulders and great physical strength. In the streets, he often stopped to show workmen how to use tools properly. He stood out because of the black stovepipe hat sitting squarely on his head at all times except when in the Church Sanctuary. His square jaw shows determination; he is a man no one takes lightly.

Figure 20 - Sketch by Officer Bill Cronley
The Informant — August 1970

The people turn to Father Donnelly in their hour of need. Not only do they trust him, but also they are positive his property would not be searched if the rebels entered the city. He will be protected as a religious man, they whispered; and it was rumored he was a friend of General Price. The afternoon shadows deepened and preparation for the approaching battle became more ominous. Groups of Father Donnelley's parishioners and many Protestant friends and merchants came up the path through a tree-covered ravine to the priest's study and church. They brought their valuables in cans, bags, jars or any other containers available. They pleaded with Father Donnelly to take care of them until the trouble passed.

Father Donnelly related to his biographer, Father William J. Dalton, that first he shrank from the great responsibility pressed upon him. He attempted to make the people understand that war did not respect the cloth when army needs were pressing. He felt he would be no more immune from search than the rest of them. They would not listen;

women wept and begged and the men pleaded in whispering voices.

Reluctantly, Father Donnelly opened his memorandum book and began making entries. He had served as a schoolmaster before becoming a priest; he was a meticulous man. He entered the names and the amounts in a ledger with a long quill. He double-checked the amounts and the spelling of names.

As night settled about him, the line at the desk became much longer. One small lone candle shone, its uncertain light casting eerie shadows about the room. The work became even slower than before, with the good father bending so far over the ledger that his face almost touched the page. People in line grew more restless. Price was on the brink of entering the city. Some swore they could hear fighting to the south. They left their unidentified wealth on his desk and rushed out. They left with a departing glance and plea, "You take care of it Father, we must hurry back to our homes and families."

When they were gone, the priest held money and valuables without the slightest idea to whom much of it belonged. He chided himself for his foolhardiness, but he resolved to protect the wealth in his care to the best of his ability.

Now he needed a secure place to hide the money and other valuables. He thought and thought. He reasoned the graveyard would be the safest place. He searched until he found a wooden box suitable to hold the treasure. He placed the money and other valuables in it, hoisted the heavy burden upon his shoulders, and walked to the cabin of the old sexton and gravedigger named Tom.

The two men loaded the box into Tom's wheelbarrow along with the necessary digging tools. They wheeled the load into the cemetery. It was approximately two blocks west of the church. The cemetery was between Eleventh and Twelfth Streets along Pennsylvania Avenue and one hundred fifty feet west of what is now the west side of Jefferson Street.

The pale glow of their lantern danced and flickered on the tombstones like a firefly as they labored. Somewhere in the nearby woods, an owl hooted. Over on Broadway they could hear the crunching of men's marching feet, the soft whinny of horses and the braying of pack mules.

Tom dug up a grassy spot, taking care as he removed the sod and loaded the loose dirt in the wheelbarrow. They placed the box carefully in the hole. They carefully replaced the sod and swept away the remaining evidence of excavation. The job was finished. Father Donnelly returned home for a much-needed rest. Unfortunately, Tom, the Sexton, did not go home. He went instead to a crowded saloon at Eighth and Main Streets. After a few shots of whiskey, the sexton's tongue could not hold the secret.

"It was a good thing indeed, the good father and I have done this night," he related to the fascinated crowd. "Never has any man in this room laid eyes on such a treasure as we

Figure 21 - Sketch by Officer Bill Cronley
The Informant — August 1970

buried in the little cemetery upon the hill."

Word of Tom's loose tongue soon reached Father Donnelly. He lost no time in recruiting four trusted men. Armed and under cover of darkness, the five men went to the little cemetery. They dug up the box. They buried it the second time just behind the Church of the Immaculate Conception. The church faced Broadway between Eleventh and Twelfth Streets. The job finished, Father Donnelly again retired, but sleep eluded him. He was very restless. He kept asking himself how he could trust four men when he had found it impossible to trust one.

He again crawled from his bed and again shouldered his shovel. This time he would trust only himself. He once again took the box from its hiding place. This time he carefully stepped off paces, starting at the corner of the church. He started to the north noting first one landmark then pacing off another, recording it in his book, and then pacing off the distance to the next. Almost exhausted, Father Donnelly again buried his charge. Its last resting place was under a large tree. The leaves of autumn rustled with the early morning breeze. The first beam of light had not yet appeared but the sounds of night were fast fading. He returned to the parish house, carefully cleaned and replaced his tools, then retired to the restful sleep of an unworried man. The next day the Battle of Westport started with all its bloody fury. Father Donnelly served three days on the battlefield without rest. He served as chaplain for both the blue and the gray with written permission to tend the wounded and bury the dead. He administered rites to the dying and knelt on roughhewn, blood soaked floors to nurse the wounded in homes surrounding the battlefield. When General Price retreated, Father Donnelly arranged for the wounded of both sides to be cared for in private homes in Westport, Kansas City, and Independence.

One month later, Father Donnelly was able to continue with his parish duties. He thought it was time to recover

Figure 22 - Sketch by Officer Bill Cronley
The Informant — August 1970

and return the treasure left with him in trust. He shouldered his shovel, consulted his logbook, and went to the hiding place. With care, he stepped off the distance between points as he had recorded them. He dug very carefully, expecting his shovel to strike a firm object. This did not happen. His shovel struck only soft earth. He was becoming most apprehensive. He measured and dug again; then again. He became more rattled in his digging. Where had he last buried the elusive treasure? Father Donnelly was unsure of the location. In later years when relating the story, he recalled that it was a remote spot some distance from the second hiding place.

The next night he again attempted to locate the site. He returned home knowing he would not find it. Something had gone amiss. Had he made a mistake in recording the location? Was he followed that morning? Did someone watch as he labored to bury the box? Then, or sometime in the hectic days that followed, was it stolen?

The cemetery where Father Donnelly first buried the treasure, a block south of Quality Hill, no longer exists. The graves were moved. The large mansions, which replaced the little cemetery, have long since given way to modern changes. When all hope of finding the lost treasure faded, Father Donnelly went to a banker and borrowed on land he owned to repay all claims. Just before Father Donnelley's death, he was delirious and sick with fever. His nurse, while checking his room, found him missing. A search found him in the cemetery. He was out of his head from his illness, but he was still searching for the lost treasure he had so carefully hidden. He was still trying to solve the mystery of what went wrong in October of 1864.

Figure 23 - Father Donnelly
Photo: Hugh Chase Private Library

BASEBALL

ON AUGUST 12, 1866, the sporting event of the year took place. It was, and would be, talked about, made legion, and discussed for many years. It was a baseball game played between the Kansas City Antelopes and Atchison Pomeroys. It was a playoff for the Missouri Valley Baseball championship. The game lasted two hours and fifty-three minutes. It ended with the score Kansas City 48 and Atchison 28.

The game had the distinction of being part of the legends that surrounded Jim "Wild Bill" Hickok and Chief Thomas Speers of the Kansas City Missouri Police Department. Several men walked from the police station across the market square to enter Mr. Focade's saloon at Fourth and Main Streets. From behind the bar, Mr. Focade called to a man sitting at the poker table. "Jim, you expecting callers?" This man, whom people knew as "Wild Bill Hickok," was playing poker with one of the city fathers. At that time, "Wild Bill" was a United States Deputy Marshal assigned to the Kansas City area. He wore a long deerskin suit, with his six shooters tucked into a fancy hand-made sash about his waist.

The men entered, led by Chief Tom Speers. "This a posse?" asked Hickok. "No, baseball," answered Chief Speers. "These gentlemen are officers of the Kansas City Antelopes, Mr. Twitchell, President, Mr. Warner, vice-president, and Mr. Winants, secretary." They shook hands, then the Chief introduced a man in a fancy frock coat and striped baggy pants known as Mr. Bliss.

Mr. Twitchell started relating about the ballgame the week before. He explained that the Kansas City group of fellers had learned to like baseball during the Civil War and made up their own team. They did well, too. They were winning up and down the Missouri River Valley until they went to Atchison to play for the championship. They had their pants beaten off them by the Atchison Pomeroys, Mr. Bliss' team. They played the game last week in Kansas City; Kansas City won.

"Maybe we should have and maybe we shouldn't have," Mr. Twitchell said. "The Pomeroys complained that the crowd was rowdy and unfriendly. It may have been that it was." Mr. Bliss interrupted, "Could have been! Could have been! Every time one of our players would go after a fly ball, somebody would start shooting a gun in the air. Then if the umpire said the wrong thing, 'bang!' would go those six guns again! Poor guy took off before the game ended. He must be

Figure 24 — Sketch of "Wild Bill" Hickok
Sketch: Hugh Chase Private Library

running yet. As for us, some of our folks got upset too. There was a lot of pushin' and shoving."

"I'll say," spoke up the Chief. "Took a string of wagons guarded by my boys to get the Atchison folks back to the riverboat." Mr. Bliss spoke up again, "We would like to play one more game so we will know who is really champion." Mr. Twitchell nodded. "We would like to play next Saturday afternoon. Only this time we are determined to have order. Will you umpire for us, Mr. Hickok?"

Wild Bill poured himself a drink, took a long sip and sat in deep thought for a few seconds. "That would depend on the rules," he stated. "Do you play by the knickerbockers rules?" "What's that?" asked Mr. Focade. "It's the rules that a dude ball team of New Yorkers set down. Good and fair they are," answered Hickok. "Oh, yes," said Twitchell. "We belong to the northwest association of ball players. We joined last Christmas at Chicago. They follow the knickerbockers rules." "Got a copy?" asked Hickok. "I'll brush up on them." "Then you will umpire the game?" asked Mr. Bliss, "and you will be fair?" Wild Bill smiled faintly. "I'm a U.S. Deputy Marshal, not one of the local men. I have friends here just as I have friends in Atchison. You have no call to fret." "No offense," said Mr. Bliss. "Guess I haven't recovered from the guy who umpired the last game."

Word spread fast that Wild Bill Hickok would be the official at the ballgame. People who had been afraid decided they could safely take their families to the game. Saturday, the day of this important game, arrived. The playing field was located at Fourteenth Street between what is now Oak and Locust Streets. It sloped from east to west then leveled out to what is Grand Avenue today. No tickets were sold and spectators sat where they could find space. Even the animals, hitched and standing outside the area, seemed to reflect the festivities.

The crowd cheered as Mr. Hickok strode onto the diamond shaped playing field. He took his place by first base.

Figure 25 - Sketch by Officer Bill Cronley
The Informant – July 1970

He wore a bright red sash about his waist with his pistols tucked in place. The rules were somewhat different than we know them in modern baseball. The pitcher was required to pitch underhanded. The batter requested if he wanted to be pitched high or low. The pitcher had to keep throwing until the batter had taken three swings. A base on balls, or the strike zone, had never been heard of.

Mr. Hickok tossed a quarter high in the air. The Pomeroys won the toss and batted first. The bats were long, thick and heavy. A fielder attempted to catch the ball in flight or on the first bounce. No one wore a glove.

During the second inning, the Kansas City catcher hit a fly ball over the fence. A Pomeroy player moved back to catch it on the fly. Two shots echoed through the air. The player made the catch but everything else became silent. The crowd froze.

Mr. Hickok patted his pistols slowly and walked in the direction of the shots. Seconds later, he returned to his job as umpire. As he was returning, he handed two pistols to Chief Speers, which he confiscated from two over-zealous fans. The game continued.

Kansas City won the game fair and square. The crowd let out a big cheer as Mr. Bliss unwrapped a shiny new baseball and presented it to Mr. Twitchell, the custom of that time. Mr. Twitchell then asked Mr. Hickok how he could be paid for the excellent service he had rendered. "Send to the livery stable for an open carriage pulled by two white horses and deliver me back to town," said Wild Bill. This wish was carried out. The crowd then dispersed with everyone feeling they witnessed a fair and well-played contest.

ANNIE CHAMBERS

A TWENTY-FIVE ROOM MANSION once stood at the corner of Third and Wyandotte Streets. The palatial furnishings matched the elegance of a castle. The furnishings reflected every known comfort and convenience imagined by interior decorators or architects of that era, including a spacious ballroom. This estate was the home and business location of a woman who, in the early days of Kansas City, was very well known. This woman almost became a legend in her time. For a better understanding of the individual and the house that stood on this site, one must look far back in this lady's past.

Annie Chambers was born on June 6, 1842, in Lexington, Kentucky. Annie must have possessed more than an average amount of innocent beauty as a young lady. Abraham Lincoln asked her to ride with him in a political parade when making his first bid for presidency. Being young, Annie jumped at the chance to show off her charms in such distinguished company. Her father, a true Southerner, felt disgraced at the implication that members of his family supported a Yankee. I tell this story only to date Annie in the era in which she lived. Annie became a schoolteacher and soon met and married her husband, a man by the name of William Chambers. Their first child lived less than one year. Annie was in her second pregnancy when she fell while going for a buggy ride. The accident left her in a coma for three days and caused her baby to be stillborn. Annie's husband fell to his death from a railroad trestle shortly after the loss of this baby.

The sorrow of the double tragedy left Annie with a strange outlook. She left Kentucky and moved to the north. She made a vow to herself that her life would be a short but merry one. Annie resided in Indiana for a short time. While in Indianapolis, Annie adopted a new profession. She became a prostitute, apparently by intent. She soon found herself involved and in love with one of her patrons. He was a handsome dashing blade and they discussed marriage. As it turned out, only Annie was serious. She had to learn a lesson in cruelty that went hand in hand with her chosen profession. Annie was to come face to face with her suitor's wife and children. The tale turned out as one might expect a dime novel to read. The wife pleaded with Annie to leave Indiana so that she could win her husband back. Annie, disillusioned with her lover, assented to the wife's pleas.

In 1869, Annie made the move to Kansas City. She opened her first sporting house in an area north of the Missouri River in what was then the Harlem area. Annie was the proprietress of this pleasure palace, and it soon was touted as the best in the west. Her house soon became known as a

Figure 26
Youthful Annie Chambers
Photo: Watermark Press in Wichita, Kansas

resort, with Annie as the trusted keeper.

Annie had been here but a short time when she made a shrewd observation. The city was growing, but the people who spent money on a good time were not coming north. The city was growing and spreading to the south. She decided to move in that direction with the flow since she had a sharp mind for business. Records indicate that she moved to the large mansion at Third and Wyandotte in either 1871 or 1872. She operated her brothel at that location until the WWI era. That corner was not long in gaining a reputation among the cattlemen and throughout the southwestern part of the United States as the heart of Kansas City's scarlet district.

Annie ran a strict house and the girls who worked for her could neither smoke nor drink in the parlor. The rooms upstairs were for such entertainment and there were no restrictions imposed behind closed doors. She maintained that her girls should not only act like, but also be, ladies. Any other type of behavior would give her house a bad name.

It was reliably reported that Annie did not encourage girls to take up the profession of prostitution. Whenever a girl wanted to leave, Annie would go all out to help her leave.

Any customer who found himself with more cash than was wise to carry entrusted Annie with that cash. They knew every penny would be there when reclaimed. People in polite society who took advantage of this extra rendered by her "resort" referred to her as "the banker."

The City Union Mission stood next door, a mansion almost as large as Annie's own. The Reverend and Mrs. Buckley ran this Mission. The purpose of the mission was to rehabilitate alcoholics, thieves, and men in general who were misfits in society in one way or another. They worked to give hope to these people until they found themselves and embarked again on a productive way of life.

One morning Mrs. Buckley answered a knock at the door of the mission. She was surprised and shocked to find a girl who worked for Annie standing there weeping and sobbing.

She stood in the door staring with glassy, tear-filled eyes. She stood there timidly for several seconds, and then blurted out, "My baby is dead." This baby had been born without the benefit of a father to give it a name. The peaked young lady had no idea who the father might be. She had bestowed all the love in her love-starved heart upon that tiny infant. After the baby died, she had kept the tiny body in her room until the other women convinced her the baby must be buried. She then went to Mrs. Buckley.

"My baby was never bad," she said. "I am down and out. No woman has ever lived a more sinful, wicked life than I have. My baby was good and I want her buried like any other good baby. Do you think Mr. Buckley will preach a proper funeral over my baby?"

"Yes, I am sure he would be most happy to," answered Mrs. Buckley. The tiny coffin containing the magdalene's baby rested in what had been the parlor of the mission. It stood under the crystal chandelier that seemed so out of place in the surroundings.

The mother of the baby and many down-and-outers who were patrons of the Mission gathered and knelt beside the tiny pine box, along with the scarlet ladies who were friends of the mother. The Reverend David Buckley started to speak softly over the tiny body.

Another person that this group was unaware of listened and mourned in silence at Reverend Buckley's sermon. The plush old mansion belonging to Annie Chambers almost abutted the mission. Annie stood with her hands twisted and knotted with age. She stood, showing the pain of rheumatism and arthritis, nearly blind … alone in her big house. She sat alone with her memories in that gaudy, darkened ballroom. Annie had climbed a back stairway to reach a back window when the hour of the funeral arrived. She quietly and gently raised the window so that no one would hear. She stood there calmly and silently, sobbing to herself. This was the first religious service Annie had listened to in sev-

Figure 27
Mature
Annie Chambers
Kansas City
Public Library
Special Collection

enty-five years. Annie was deeply moved as she listened to Mr. Buckley's sermon in the City Union Mission. Perhaps her mind wandered back to the time she had lost her own two children. At any rate, this experience seemed to bring about a great change in Annie, both spiritually and emotionally.

With the passage of time, the citizens of Kansas City failed to see the honor in the widespread fame of the City's scarlet district. Annie Chambers was the chief contributor to this fame.

In 1921, the mansion that had sat so proudly at Third and Wyandotte was supposedly locked for all time. However, Annie was determined to re-open. She accomplished this in 1923, and then closed again almost immediately. This time she closed the big house of her own volition.

Around 1923, Annie operated her mansion as a legitimate boarding house. Her boarders were mostly railroad employees and transient workers who traveled in and out of Kansas City.

While operating the old mansion as a boarding house

Figure 28 — Annie Chambers' House (center), City Union Mission (left). *Hugh Chase Private Library.*

Annie became close friends with Reverend and Mrs. Buckley. The Buckleys had a lot of influence in causing Annie to choose a different way of living. Annie made a great effort to live a life she felt would be pleasing to her God.

Annie Chambers passed away around seven o'clock on the morning of March 4, 1935. She was blind, ill and suffered from the usual symptoms coming with old age. However, she seemed to be at peace in the happiness she had found in her religion gained in February of 1934.

Annie slipped away to death and left this world and the once plush mansion with its many secrets. Annie left her large house to the Reverend and Mrs. David Buckley to be used in his work as he carried on with the City Union Mission.

The old mansion, with its many memories and secrets, gave way to the wrecking crew who razed the house in 1945, eleven years after Annie's death.

City Union Mission still serves God and man through their generosity in the Kansas City area.

HANNIBAL BRIDGE

IF YOU TRAVEL NORTH on Broadway to the Missouri River, it would take little more than a glance to understand how vital modern transportation is to the life of this metropolis. Looking to the north one would see two ultra-modern airports in full operation twenty-four hours a day with air traffic arriving and departing every few minutes around the clock. Looking to the south brings into view modern inter-state highways with arteries spreading in all directions, like a spider web, to carry traffic into and away from the city with ease. If you should then look up and down the Missouri River, you might see a large diesel-powered riverboat pushing several barges, cutting its way through the water.

If we were to take a closer look, we would notice the old Hannibal Bridge, stretching across the Missouri River from bank to bank. This bridge gets little use today, but we can see it is still using the railroad tracks of the lower level to carry freight. This bridge might well be considered the cornerstone of the growth of this great city and the commerce it enjoys today.

If possible to travel back in time to July 3, 1869, we would find ourselves caught up in the excitement and anticipation that hung over Kansas City and the surrounding communities. People came into the city from all directions, some traveling many miles. They wanted to be in Kansas City so they could see the first train to arrive from the north. The new bridge was complete, the first ever to stretch across the Missouri River. Tomorrow it would open.

Figure 29 — Close-up, Hannibal Bridge
Photo: Hugh Chase Private Library

This bridge was the finest in the history of this young nation. The people fell just short of idolizing it. Aging copies of the "Kansas City Times" of July 4, 1869, reflect the attitude of the citizens toward the bridge. Ten of the paper's thirty-two column edition describe and celebrate the bridge. The story praised the bridge and its builders—"The Immortal Bridge." They referred to it as "a gigantic troth" plighted by science for the future growth and expansion of Kansas City.

The crowds began to gather so early in the morning that many of the men had dew in their beards. They gathered long before the celebration commenced. People completely lined the bluffs along the river. A slight shower fell a bit earlier and the humidity was very high, but the excitement overpowered any discomfort. Marshal General Hough and his assistants organized a line of carriages, omnibuses, buggies, horsemen and footmen to start the festivities. They made their way to witness the test of the massive fabric of wood and iron that spanned the unruly river bank to bank. What a great boon to travel and commerce!

Locomotives and trains of cars passed forward and backward, testing the bridge without the slightest jar or vibration. The scene was most inspiring; a long procession, headed by the richly uniformed Knights of Templar of the Masonic Order, made their way across the river. Military bands filled the air with stirring music; the approach to the bridge was crowded with many people and vehicles. The population on the hill was estimated to be between thirty and forty thousand.

The official parade, headed by the Lafayette Silver Cornet Band, marched from Fifth Street. The parade had to halt; for at the time coming across the new bridge, was a highly decorated train. Some of the waiting thousands were haunted with a fear that the bridge would either buck around and throw the train or it would collapse completely. There was

Figure 30 — Sketch by Officer Bill Cronley
The Informant — October 1970

not even a slight quiver. The train, made up of ten cars pulled by the proud engine Hannibal, entered the bridge from the northern bank. Hidden in flags, festooned, and illuminated with flowers, the train majestically approached. Two of the cars were A. B. Pullman's celebrated sleeping cars.

The parade then crossed the river by way of the new bridge. Thousands of people swarmed down from their perch on the hill and halted on the north side of the river. There they gathered around platforms to hear speeches from General Warwick and other dignitaries.

A short time later, they heard the whistle of a steamboat and saw it from the bridge—its prow proudly cutting through the water, making her way toward the bridge. Four men manned the levers and the mighty arms of the draw swung around until the bridge rested on the supports in the middle of the river. The proud steamboat sailed gracefully between piers two and three. A roaring cheer went up from the crowd on the hill and the deck of the beautiful steamer. After the

Figure 31 — Hannibal Bridge

Photo: Hugh Chase Private Library

steamer passed by, everyone felt the bridge was a gigantic success.

This did not mark the end of the celebration. Down the levy opposite the Gillis House, R. H. Holman, a fearless aeronaut, held his balloon in check awaiting the signal to make his ascension. The time came at last. The sky mariner, after leaving the bridge two miles below him, landed two miles east of Independence, Missouri. The celebrators then reformed and marched to the barbeque ground. This was located in the pasture of Colonel E. Steen, near what are now Twelfth Street and Troost Avenue. Speeches, music, and entertainment continued late into the evening. July 4, 1869—what a day to remember!

BOB POTEE

DURING THE EARLY DAYS, before gambling became illegal and Kansas City was a young upstart community, gambling flourished wildly in this frontier town. A man could play almost any game he chose — dice, poker, roulette, etc. It was easy to find any game of chance, where one could win or lose money. One game very popular among the cattlemen west of the Mississippi River was Faro. Winning in this game depended almost entirely on luck. It was so popular in the 1870's that it became known as King Faro. Kansas City was soon to be the center of King Faro's domain. It covered a six-block area of Kansas City. This section boasted more gambling houses than any other town in America. This section was often referred to as "Old Town."

On Main Street, from Second Street to Missouri Avenue, gambling halls lined the street so closely that swinging doors almost touched each other. Many prominent men, with big reputations in early American history, passed through these doors. Wild Bill Hickok, Wyatt Earp, Bat Masterson, the Younger Brothers, Frank and Jessie James, Doc Holiday, Bill Cody, many thousands of cattlemen, muleskinners, respected gentlemen, and professional gamblers mingled in this section of Kansas City. Men like these, with flashing tempers and fast guns, earned Main Street the nickname of "Battle Row."

Bob Potee earned the name of the most honest and trustworthy card dealer west of the Mississippi among these men.

He owned a gambling hall on Missouri Avenue just off Main Street, called "Faro Number Three." Not even Wild Bill Hickok, who was well known to doubt dealers, ever questioned the manner in which Potee handled a deck of cards. Potee's fingers were an artistic machine and his honesty above reproach.

Gambling in those days was a profession, and the gentlemen who claimed gambling as their profession dressed in a fashion as indicative as a uniform. Most dressed in light colored coats and wide brimmed hats made of felt. Bob Potee always stood out as he wore a black long tailed coat, a tall silk hat and was never without his gold-headed cane. Players respected him and often talked about his "fair hands" and "square deal," but his intimate friends loved him because of his kindness and concern for the welfare of others.

Serious trouble was unheard of in Faro Number Three. The words "cheat, cold deck or misdeal" were seldom heard. Bob managed to run a quiet establishment and left fights and fist-a-cuffs to the rougher, more uncouth gambling halls in Old Town.

There was one evening in Faro Number Three remembered and discussed around campfires and on the riverboats along the Missouri River. Players filled the table around Potee. His hands were busy dealing the cards deftly in his usual quick smooth manner. Potee sat beneath overhead lamps. The others sat just inside the circle of light with their hands in plain sight. One man, a gambler unknown to the rest of the group, was donating his money at a steady flow. The drinks began to make him somewhat reckless. He still bet every hand like a true gambler. He confidently bet each turn of the cards. When he ran out of ready cash, he gave Bob his note. Potee planned to close the loser out after one more hand if he failed to win. A heavy hush settled over the room and a crowd gathered about the game in order to witness the outcome. The gambler's fingers swiftly manipulated the cards. He dealt them smoothly across the green velvet table.

The other players began placing their bets as the turn came to them. When it was the stranger's turn to place his bet, he stated in a loud voice, "This deuce didn't come from that deck, Mr. Dealer." With a grin spreading across his face, Mr. Potee laid his cards face down and turned his full attention to the stranger. "I believe you are mistaken, sir." "No," the stranger lashed out in an angry tone, "I saw you shuffle this deuce from the bottom of the deal." With this remark the man was on his feet, clawing at a side holster for a revolver.

Potee placed his hands on the table, looking into the barrel of a Navy Colt .45 and the eyes of the stranger. "Spread that deck out," shouted the angry gambler. "Sir," said Potee slowly and deliberately, "cheating is a word never used in the same sentence with my name. It is a word neither gentlemen nor thieves use in my presence." The man holding the gun again demanded the deck be spread out. Potee refused. The man's fingers turned white as they clawed at the trigger. There were two quick shots, one striking the lamp shattering it to pieces. They heard much scuffling and shouting in the dark. They heard someone dash through the front door and into the street.

It wasn't long until the lamp was replaced, flooding a circle of light on the table. The strong stench of gunpowder filled the air. Bob Potee sat with his hands still on the tabletop. The body of the stranger slumped dead on the floor in a half kneeling position at the edge of the card table. "New hand being dealt," announced Bob as the body was carried from the room; Potee dealt the cards as King Faro continued to reign in Old Town, Kansas City. Bob Potee always claimed that gambling and society were two elements that could not co-exist peaceably. He was well aware that one, in time, would bring an end to the other. Potee was not even a little surprised when the government instituted the Johnson Anti-Gambling Act of 1881. He had felt it coming. He knew that the gamblers' aristocracy was ending. King Faro would be dethroned. Men started drifting to satisfy their gambling habit, with the law close behind them. Bob Potee stuck with Faro Number Three. He did not budge. He sat quietly at his table watching "Old Town" die.

Shortly Potee made a decision. He dressed, donning one of his finest suits, placed his tall silk hat on his head, took a firm grip on his gold-headed cane and strolled across the street to a neighboring gambling hall. He left a note for his close friend, Joe Bassett. He then strolled north on Main Street. He cheerfully tipped his silk hat to friends passing. He proudly straightened his shoulders and smiled at passer-bys. He strolled down the hill past Second Street, across First Street, then casually and with proud dignity, walked toward the center of the Missouri River until only his tall silk hat could be seen. It floated downstream — never recovered.

He left instructions in the note to his friend, Joe Bassett. It read, "Plant me decently, Joe." Joe carried out his wish. Samuel Booktaver delivered the sermon in the Grand Avenue Church that made "Old Town" shed tears. Six tall gamblers carried the mahogany casket to a private lot where Bob Potee was given over to the earth. That brought an end to a man, an era, and a way of life that would never return.

GEORGE CALEB BINGHAM

GEORGE CALEB BINGHAM, world-famous artist, was a member of the first Board of Police Commissioners in Kansas City, Missouri. The first board formed in 1874. The Metropolitan Police Law established Kansas City's Police Department, and Governor Charles Hardin appointed the first Board of Police Commissioners. They were George Caleb Bingham, W. M. McDearmon and H. J. Latshaw.

They held their first meeting April 11, 1874 to organize the Commission. They elected H. J. Latshaw as President of the new board. He quickly gave up the office for undisclosed reasons. At the next meeting, held April 15, 1874, George Caleb Bingham became the Board President and set about to organize and build the newly founded department.

George C. Bingham displayed his interest in the community long before that when Missouri had problems as a border state during the War Between the States. Those days were difficult for Kansas City and neighboring communities. The Civil War split the nation and caused families to turn on each other. In 1863, General Thomas Ewing, Jr. issued the infamous "Order No. 11"; it was an order that was to haunt him the rest of his life. "Order No. 11" stated that all persons living in Cass, Bates and parts of Vernon County in Missouri were to vacate their homes within fifteen days. The act that precipitated Order No. 11 was a simple one. It began one hot afternoon in August 1863. A woman, long forgotten, rushed up to a Union soldier and pointed to a buggy occupied by two women. She whispered to the soldier that these women were wives of rebels and that they were feeding secessionists and members of Quantrell's guerrillas. The Union Army arrested and imprisoned the two women. One of the women was Mrs. Charity Kerr, sister of one of Quantrell's raiders. The other woman was her widowed sister-in-law, Mrs. Nanie McCorkle. The army held them prisoner at 1409 Grand Avenue in a section called McGee's addition. They were placed in custody and held with seven other women, known Southern sympathizers, who fed rebels and guerillas. Tempers flared that August on both sides of the state line. The Jayhawkers raided the Missouri side; Quantrell plundered the Kansas side. What happened to those women prisoners only served to increase the tension. George Bingham, a Union man, expressed doubt about the safety of the building in which they were held. His fears

Figure 32 — Order No. 11, Housed for many years at Nelson Art Gallery. Now housed at National Gallery of Art, Washington, D.C. *Photo: Kansas City Public Library Special Collection.*

were justified; the building collapsed. Four women died, including Mrs. Kerr. Enraged, Quantrell's raiders carried out their revenge by sacking Lawrence, Kansas. One hundred and seventy people met their death in that raid.

The Union retaliated. Major John M. Shofield, Union Commander, reluctantly agreed to the seizure or destruction of the homes of disloyal persons. On August 25, 1863, General Ewing issued Order No. 11. He commanded all companies and attachments to carry out this order. George Bingham spoke out loudly against the order. He even made a trip to Jefferson City to protest the order. He again pleaded with General Ewing to rescind the order. When General Ewing refused to do so, Bingham stomped from his office shouting in rage, "I will make you infamous on canvas!"

Bingham watched the order carried out. He observed good loyal men shot down, and women patching together improvised wagons, hitching wild calves to them in place of horses. All horse and wagons serviceable or usable were confiscated. Some families left, never to return, since the order affected loyal and confederate sympathizers alike. The exodus left the countryside free for more plunder and destruction.

From his eyewitness experience, Bingham painted Order No. 11. The painting was originally called "Martial Law." The canvas depicted the cruel treatment and abuse the people received at the hands of the Union Soldiers. Bingham maintained a lifelong campaign against General Ewing. Long after the war, General Ewing entered Ohio politics. He was a representative in the U.S. Congress and he sought the Governorship as a stepping-stone toward a presidential candidacy. Bingham sent copies of his painting and letters damning the war to Ewing's opponents. Ewing never received the governorship. Bingham's painting, "Order No. 11," hung for many years in the Nelson Art Gallery. It is currently on display at the National Gallery of Art in Washington, D.C.

Figure 33
George Caleb Bingham
Photo:
Hugh Chase Private Library

THOMAS M. SPEERS

IN THE YEAR 1874, Marshal Thomas M. Speers became the first Chief of Police of Kansas City, Missouri, under the new State Metropolitan Police Law. He was only twenty-nine years old. Thomas M. Speers was a contemporary of Wyatt Earp, Bat Masterson, Doc Holiday, "Wild Bill" Hickok, and other well-known servants of the gun. He had twenty-eight men in his police department — twenty-two patrolmen, one turnkey, two detectives, two sergeants, one captain and himself.

Thomas M. Speers was one of the most popular and famous law enforcement officers in the history of the city. His ideas and policy put him years ahead of his time. Speers, a man of medium height with broad shoulders, appeared much stouter than the average man. He was a native of Missouri, born near St. Louis in 1839. His parents resided in Missouri when it was a territory. They crossed the Mississippi River and settled on a Spanish land grant purchased by his grandfather in 1811. Being a young man who loved adventure, the lure of gold took Tom Speers to California at the ripe age of sixteen. The same call of adventure in five years found him a member of the San Francisco Vigilance Committee under the leadership of the famous William T. Coleman.

He returned to St. Louis in 1859 to join his father in a brick manufacturing business. In 1868, he came to Kansas City to set up a brick business. He soon gave up business to enter politics. In 1870, he was elected the town marshal of

Figure 34
Youthful Thomas Speers
Photo:
Hugh Chase Private Library

Kansas City. In 1874, the Metropolitan Police Law established Kansas City's Police Department. Governor Charles Hardin appointed George Caleb Bingham, famous

Figure 35
Mature Chief Speers
Photo: Hugh Chase
Private Library

Missouri artist, W. M. McDearmon and H. J. Latshaw as the first Board of Police Commissioners. Bingham became the first president of the board and led to the selection of Speers as the first Chief of Police of Kansas City. He held this post twenty-one years, the longest any Chief ever served this community.

Speer's policy was, when possible, to prevent crime rather than apprehend the offender. His police department picked up known criminals when they arrived in town. He detained them until the first roll call, and his officers had a look at them (possibly the first line-up). The police released them with a warning of arrest if seen in town after a specified time. They were also cautioned they would be strong suspects in any crimes occurring while they were in town.

Figure 36 — Lawmen and gunmen of Chief Speers era (Top row) W.H. Harris, Luke Short, Bat Masterson. (Sitting) Charlie Bassett, Wyatt Earp, L. McLean, Neal Brown
Photo: Epoch Collection
Postcard: Hugh Chase Private Library

Figure 37 — Unidentified police officers, Chief Speers far right
Photo: Hugh Chase Private Library

Speers was removed from office in 1895 apparently because of his part in unmasking the malfeasance of a Justice of the Peace. Governor William J. Stone ordered the Police Commissioners to replace Speers with one of his friends.

Figure 38 — Unidentified officers under Speers command
Photo: Hugh Chase Private Library

The Police Commissioners refused the order, and then resigned. Governor Stone appointed new commissioners, and they removed Speers from office May 4, 1895. The Governor appointed L.R. Irwin Chief.

Speers died March 20, 1896, less than a year after removal from office. At the time of his death, he was one of the best-known, most respected men in Kansas City. He was mentioned several times as a candidate for Mayor.

Restructure

APRIL 15, 1874, was a very important day for Kansas City. This is the day recognized as the first official steps taken to organize the Metropolitan Police Department of Kansas City, Missouri. The Board of Police Commissioners mapped out a strategy necessary to begin a successful police organization. Five days later the City Marshal turned his office over to the newly appointed Chief of Police, Tom Speers. The Chief filed his oath, as did Captain McQueeny and Sergeant Dennis Malloy.

On April 21, 1874, all officers of the former organization, who had served as City Marshals, were released. Mr. James McKnight, upon his release as a City Marshal, was appointed to the Metropolitan Police Department as a Detective, the first in the new organization. On April 23, George A. Shumacher was selected as a Sergeant and the Board of Police Commissioners took a position on the height standard for officers. They set it at five feet and one-half inches. On May 11, the standard was reduced half an inch and two days later, the organization of the Police Department was formally adopted. The following men comprised the police force patrolmen, seven of whom remained active members of the Department until 1910:

1. Richard Steavenson
2. D. C. Snyder
3. H. E. Tryon

4. John S. Branham (later promoted to Captain)
5. James A. McMinamin
6. C. E. Fredenberg
7. John Mulholland
8. George Bryant (later promoted to Detective)
9. Martin Hynes (first Kansas City Police Officer killed in the line of duty)
10. Frank McCarty (later promoted to Detective)
11. W. B. Hanlon (later promoted to Detective)
12. John York
13. P. J. Kennedy
14. H. F. Schrump (later promoted to Sergeant)
15. P. J. Gallopy (alone broke up a train robbery gang)
16. Michael Kelly
17. Thomas Flahive (later became Chief of Police)
18. James Flanagen (later became Sergeant)
19. William F. Davis
20. Louis Tompkins (Kansas City's first black officer)
21. Daniel Quinn
22. John Brennan
23. Detective Cornelius O'Hara

From a modest beginning in 1874, keeping pace with the growth of the city, the Metropolitan Kansas City Police Department has a total of 1,225 law enforcement officers and 614 civilian employees. The Department's personnel breakdown is: one Chief, four Deputy Chiefs, sixteen Majors, forty-five Captains, no Lieutenants, one hundred ninety-six Sergeants, no Corporals, one hundred ninety-eight Detectives, seven hundred sixty-five Police officers, and twenty-five Police Officer Candidates. The Board of Police Commissioners has five members appointed by the Governor of Missouri.

L.A. TILLMAN

THROUGHOUT THE HISTORY of the Kansas City Missouri Police Department, there have been many firsts. Among those were the first black police officers in the Midwest. Between 1874 and 1903, these men were appointed to the Police Department: Louis Tompkins, Robert Alexander, and Lafayette Tillman. All three had a very different his-

Figure 39 — Louis Tompkins (left) and Lafayette A. Tillman (right). *Photos: Hugh Chase Private Library*

tory and background. Lafayette Tillman stands out among the three, especially circa 1900's. He was certainly a Kansas City pioneer with a badge.

Lafayette Tillman defied much about local life in the early years of the twentieth century. He was a college-educated black man with a badge, somehow earning the respect of a society that flocked to opera houses to chuckle at minstrels in blackface.[1]

Little is known about the career of Officer Tillman as one of the first black officers in Kansas City, Missouri. Given the events and times of 1903, he was a noticed individual in the Police Department.

Some of the events of reported violent clashes between police and impoverished African-Americans, packed into tenements east of downtown, were reported in local newspapers. A typical headline in the newspapers read, "Policeman Kills a Negro." After six white boys threw rocks at a black church during Sunday services, the preacher said, "If we can't get protection from the police…we would hate to resort to pistols and clubs."

Officer Tillman spanned the racial divide in a city roughly ten per cent black. Lafayette Tillman was born in 1859 in Indiana; he studied music at Oberlin College and attended Wayland Seminary. In the 1880's he moved with his wife Amy to Kansas City and ran a barbershop. In the city directory, he was listed as a "colored barber." Information from that time indicates that he catered to white customers and sang bass solo for white congregations.

Lafayette joined the volunteer infantry during the Spanish-American War. Tillman's appointment as a First Lieutenant in a black regiment prompted a local Democratic club, nearly all white, to present him a gleaming sword. Upon Lieutenant Tillman's return from the Philippines, "a number of influential white citizens, appreciating his patriotism

---

1 *The Kansas City Star, January 18, 1998*

and loyalty, secured a position for him on the police force," according to a 1914 obituary published after Officer Tillman's death.

ROBERT GILLHAM

ROBERT GILLHAM made the bone-jarring trip from New York to Kansas City in 1878, hoping to establish himself in the new location. He had studied and worked hard to learn his chosen profession as an engineer. Train travel had little to offer, and the trip to Kansas City was very tiring. He was planning to rest a few days before attempting to get down to business.

He arrived at the old Union Depot located at Ninth Street and Union Avenue in Kansas City's West Bottoms. He departed from the train immediately and began walking west, searching for the main part of Kansas City. Gillham walked several blocks, and then stopped a man to ask directions. He learned he was going in the opposite direction. He was seeking a location on the other side of a large bluff looming some distance to the east. He started his long hike toward the main part of the city. As he hiked, he came upon one of the mule cars that operated between the two Kansas Cities. He was exhausted from his travels and ready to settle for any type of transportation. He boarded the mule car and found the floor strewn with dirty hay. The teamster collected the fare and left the driving and the pace to the mules.

That trip from the old Union Station convinced Gillham how badly Kansas City needed his talents. As a young engineer, he decided that the need was here and he discovered the home he was seeking. He made Kansas City his home base for the rest of his life.

Robert Gillham was unable to shake the experience of his crude arrival from his mind. He knew he must find a better way of getting from the depot to the heart of Kansas City's business district. He felt the trip should be safer, easier and quicker. Gillham knew the cable system in San Francisco well. He felt the same system was made to order for conquering the bluffs and hills of Kansas City.

Gillham opened an office and took small jobs at first. He gave scrutiny to all opportunities and became acquainted with the people as well as the geography of the area. While doing this he drew plans for a new sewage system to hold pollution to a minimum. This replaced the old system, which was becoming a health hazard. After completion of the sewer, he gave more time to his pet project. He had roughed out his idea of a transit system.

Soon after Gillham explained his idea to friends, they began to make the estimated amount of money available. He soon had the necessary financing, but that turned out to be only one major problem out of the way. He was troubled

Figure 40 — Early trolley car
Photo: Hugh Chase Private Library

then with getting his franchise and convincing the city fathers to widen Ninth Street, which at that time was only forty-eight feet wide. He also had to defeat opposition of the horse-car operators already in business.

When Robert Gillham felt ready to start construction of his project, he found new difficulties regarding patents on the grip device he planned to use. The cable car operator latched and gripped onto the moving cable between the rails to pull the car along using this device. This grip was patent protected and held in trust. Gillham felt the royalties were too expensive and soon invented a grip of his own.

When the project was completed and ready to begin operation, Gillham received an injury from the equipment that nearly took his life. He was in the inspection pit of the cable car house and power plant checking one of the grips when a piece of equipment fell, striking him on the head. He suffered two fractures the length of his skull. Gillham left the launching of his system to others, but he made medical history. He underwent surgery almost unheard of at that time. Doctors inserted a silver plate in his skull and he made a miraculous recovery.

His next major project was an elevated railway from the Union Depot to Kansas City, Kansas. D. H. Edgerton promoted this venture. Mr. Edgerton came to the area in connection with building the Union Pacific Railroad.

After Gillham's cable line was in operation for a time, he could see its shortcomings. He was unhappy with the steep incline and he decided the Eighth Street tunnel was the solution for his problems. Many men talked of the tunnel, but they only dreamed. Gillham started work constructing the tunnel through the bluff. This tunnel remained in use until 1957.

Robert Gillham built public transportation in many cities. He also engineered the canal that enabled Port Arthur, Texas to become a thriving seaport. He laid out streetcar lines and assisted in establishing transportation companies in Boston, Massachusetts; Denver, Colorado; Omaha, Nebraska; Cleveland, Ohio; Fort Worth, Texas; Providence, Rhode Island; Nashville, Tennessee; St. Joseph, Missouri; Scranton, Pennsylvania, and other cities. He also owned the city's only iron foundry and was the engineer who built Kansas City's Belt Railway. It is now the Kansas City Terminal Railroad, and the Kansas City, Pittsburg and Gulf Railroad became the Kansas City Southern Railway.

Robert Gillham died at the young age of forty-four years from pneumonia and appendicitis. Kansas City remembers him as one of her outstanding citizens with the gift of achieving the impossible.

QUALITY HILL

CLARK'S POINT is one spot in Kansas City where one might watch the mighty Missouri River as it proudly and majestically turns to the east in its long journey to St. Louis. It then turns south to the Gulf of Mexico. From this vantage, one can also watch the Kansas River as it is swallowed and becomes part of the mighty Missouri. This spot is Quality Hill. It stands high above this natural picture of intense activity. Progress brings the construction of new buildings, remodeling of some, and razing of others. Look to the Bottoms to the west for a panoramic view that reveals a city's life. From this view, one can see warehouses, cattle runs, bridges, two great airports and railroad tracks reaching thousands of miles in every direction.

At one time, a person would see only the two great rivers winding their way through a rich forest of trees. Just prior to the Civil War, Kersey Coates saw this inspiring scene. He considered it a smart business move to buy land on this hill, and he envisioned that one day it would become an important part of a great city. Kersey Coates was different from most men — he lived to see his dream come alive.

The years of the Civil War brought disaster to this small village at the bend in the river. The struggle for existence was hard. The tragedy of brother fighting brother occurred within the city limits. When the war ended, Kansas City had an extremely rough period of reconstruction. It suffered through all the bitterness and travail attending that period of history. The nation was moving westward, and the tiny community in the bend of the river began to grow. A multitude of people flocked to Kansas City seeking fortunes. In 1880, Kansas City had grown to boast a population of over one hundred thousand.

Hostilities from the Civil War necessitated that those migrating to Kansas City from the south and from the north live in separate sections of the city. Main Street served as the Mason Dixon line. The southerners located in the broad section to the east, while those from the north and east chose the territory to the west. This created the birth of Quality Hill. At that time, the heart of the business district was Ninth and Main Street. Residents found themselves confined by the bluff on the west and north — Eleventh Street on the south and Central on the east. Soon the insight of Kersey Coates began to show. The property he acquired prior to the war was in great demand. Large mansions like those seen in New England began to show up in the neighborhood. It was as sedate as it was elegant. Horse and carriage was the transportation of the day. The cable car had not made its appearance. It was a time when rigid rules and compliance of etiquette was expected. All entertainment took place in the homes; it was there that protocol demanded a young blade court his best girl.

The decline and run-down condition of Quality Hill started before the Twentieth Century. The beautiful gardens, shade trees, and the easy carefree life gave way to a faster pace. Families moved to the rural country on Armour and Quality Hill's decline was rapid. A few die-hard families chose to stay. The district suffered distress and the once splendid old mansions became ruins. It looked as if Kansas City no longer needed Quality Hill. Deterioration became even greater as the years passed, and need for the district became less.

One day Quality Hill was rediscovered. Time had taken a toll on the once proud, but now tired, old mansions. They were beyond repair. Many were torn down and in their place now stands a cluster of magnificent modern apartment buildings. They perch proudly on the bluff, commanding a view not found in any other location in the city. This restoration with the modern buildings brings new life to Quality Hill and Kansas City.

Figure 41 — Quality Hill, ca. 1886
Photo: Kansas City Public Library Special Collections

JACKASS MAIL

IT IS THE YEAR 1880. Imagine yourself making a trip with young James Brice, carrying the mail from Independence to Santa Fe, New Mexico. It is winter; the temperature is hanging around ten degrees above zero and the ground is covered in six inches of sparkling snow. You travel out to North Terrace Park, a dry airy spot that is a target for the stiff north wind. You sweep away the snow from a space six feet square and spread a fur robe and a blanket on the heavy brown grass. Now you roll up in another blanket or two and go to sleep. You wake the next morning, start a fire of dried grass, fry some salt pork, and boil some coffee. After breakfast, you break camp, start on a thirty-mile trek over country as cold and open as the site where you spent the night. Do that every day for three weeks for a salary of fifty dollars a month. This should give you a mental picture of the life Jim Brice lived for many years as mail boy.

Jim Brice was a small man, not nearly as large as his two sons who were members of the Kansas City Police Department in the early 1900's. It was Jim Brice's habit to leave the square in Independence early Monday mornings. The firm of Hall and Porter, mail contractors, employed him. They traveled in teams consisting of two mail boys and a conductor. They planned their trip and prepared Sunday mornings by picking mules from a large herd at the Hall and Porter farm. These mules must be properly shod, harness in good condition, and wagons loaded with corn when leaving Independence. These special wagons were Murphy Wagons after the man who designed and manufactured them in St. Louis, Missouri.

When starting the trip, they used six mules, taking two extra mules for emergency use. When a mule became sick during the haul, they placed a blanket on him and threw a sack of corn on the ground for him. They always left the sick animal near water. If he lived and remained free from Indians, they picked him up on the return trip.

They carried two mail sacks; one a through sack, not opened until they reached Santa Fe, and the other a way sack. This way sack contained mail for people on the route. Olathe was the first station. Here they took the way sack in, and dumped it on the floor. The people looked through the mail, picked out what they considered theirs, then sent the rest on to the next stop, Council Grove. Here they again took the sack from the wagon and repeated the procedure. They also changed mules there and picked up a lighter wagon. Fort Union was the next stop — then on to Dodge City, Kansas.

Below Dodge City, they traveled through a large buffalo range. In the summer, they met Indians from many tribes and many parts of the country who hunted and killed their winter meat supply. The government sent soldiers with them from there to the Arkansas River just to let the Indians know who was in control. During the hunting season, Indian tepees stretched for miles along the Arkansas River.

On one trip, they found an immigrant train attacked by the Kiowa. They buried several bodies. A poodle protected one of the bodies, keeping varmints away. They took the faithful little dog with them to the next campsite and let the little dog down. His feet hardly touched the ground when he started at full speed back over the trail they just traveled. They were unable to hold or stop him. Covering the same trail several weeks later, they found the faithful little animal dead of starvation at the grave of his master.

Figure 42 - Sketch by officer Bill Cronley
The Informant –January 1970

Barring uprisings, it was a pleasant life for a young man in the summer. The food supply was always abundant with the buffalo and antelope. Often they met the other mail wagon going the opposite direction. The contract called for weekly mail. When they met, they always set up camp together. This always called for a feast. The westbound mail passed along gossip from Independence with the eastbound crew relating news from Santa Fe. Early the next morning after exchanging good-byes they parted, heading in opposite directions.

The mail boys exchanged mules and wagons again six-hundred fifty miles or seventeen days out of Independence, Missouri. From that point on, the rest of the trip usually went smoothly. Santa Fe lay located in a valley, and at first glimpse it reminded one more of a brickyard than a city buried at the edge of civilization. It consisted of large square adobe houses. The moment a citizen of Santa Fe saw them, a cry would go out; "Eastern mail, the mail boys!" One could see the look of anxiety and anticipation on the faces upon their arrival. The once-a-week mail was of great importance to the people of Santa Fe.

If James Brice had time at the end of his twenty-one day schedule, he was allowed a week to rest in Santa Fe. He looked forward to this with great pleasure. The citizens treated him like a distinguished visitor, wining and dining him. They then started the trip home on Monday.

James Brice was born in Donegal, Ireland. He immigrated to the United States in 1857. One year after his arrival, he went to work for the mail contractor. He held this position until his retirement. James Brice passed away December 12, 1908.

RIOTS

IN THE EARLY HISTORY of Kansas City, Chief Tom Speers felt his force was able to handle any riots or emergencies. Kansas City enjoyed immunity from riots rare in the history of American cities. Perhaps the frequency of individual shootings, murder, and bloodletting when Kansas City was a border town gave the general populace a sufficient taste of blood. Perhaps those encounters preserved the balance of crime, if such a thing exists, and made way for more wholesale proceedings. On the other hand, possibly the various "scraps" resulted in a sufficient number of fatalities to prevent the accumulation of misfits forming the regular history-making variety of mob rioters. With the exception of the great railroad strikes, nothing greater than the impromptu vigilante lynching threatened the law or peace of the community.

Veteran Chief Tom Speers watched his force grow from a mere handful of untrained policemen to a large body of metropolitan officers. He proudly claimed there had never been a riot that his department could not control. This must be taken in the sense that no continuous act of violence would have been accomplished. For there had been times when the available force of men instantly controlled the avenging might of the enraged populace. However, even with that restriction the department made a marvelously good showing. The lynching of a man named Harrington in April of 1882 is a good example. Pat Jones, a blacksmith who worked on west Ninth Street, was walking down Bluff Street. He became involved in a slight altercation with two black men. One or both of the men involved shot and killed Mr. Jones. Both men fled the area of the crime. Shortly after their escape, the police arrested a black man named Harrington on suspicion of murder. The tale of the brutal murder spread like wildfire within the city. When the officers, with Mr. Harrington in custody, attempted to cross the bridge just north of the Union Depot, a mass of men and boys of nearly one thousand strong met them. The mob unceremoniously took the prisoner from the officers. Within an hour of the murder, the mob hung Mr. Harrington from a pillar of the bridge. The mob acted with speedy avenging justice to the known facts. Unfortunately, the mob had an innocent man. The real murderer proved to be George "Tony" Grant, who made his escape into Kansas. Mr. Harrington had no connection to the crime other than a scapegoat of the excited multitude.

Three railroad strikes, beginning in 1878, brought about near riots. Striking workmen completely controlled the Union Depot. They shouted threats of pillage and destruction, first in secret and then thundered aloud. This culminated one afternoon in a mob marching up Delaware Street spilling into the main thoroughfare by the hundreds. Dire threats struck fear in the hearts of the more timid, who put up their shutters and waited in expectation for more fearful developments. Content with showing their muscles, the mob dispersed with a promise to return. They did not fulfill that promise.

Merchants and their employees, who would work with the police should the mob return, immediately formed a protective company of guards. They polished rifles, dispensed ammunition, and set a guard at night. The expected hostilities never came.

The second near-riot also occurred during a railroad strike. Martin Scow and an accomplice threw a switch and derailed a train in the East Bottoms. Six police officers onboard the train acted as guards. They saw the action of the strikers, but too late to save the train. The officers gave chase as the men disappeared in a lumberyard on Lydia Avenue. One of the officers drew his revolver and shot one of the miscreants in the leg. Scow escaped arrest.

Two years later was the third strike against the Burlington Railroad. This one was considered uneventful. Chief Speers stationed his men in and around the railroad yards, where he anticipated danger. Verbal abuse was the most serious incident, and it passed with no serious uprising. They did no damage other than a delay in schedules and traffic snarls.

ROBERT T. VAN HORN

IN 1884, the leading businessmen of the newly organized Town of Kansas found themselves in an uncomfortable situation. They watched most of the trade at that time go to their sister cities, Westport or Independence. They held a meeting to find a remedy and discuss the steps needed to put their town in line for more of this business. They held this meeting in the Gillis Hotel. They decided they needed a newspaper in their community. They delegated Mr. Milton Payne to travel to St. Louis to purchase equipment needed to publish a newspaper.

They gave the task of printing the paper to a journeyman printer, David K. Abeel. They delegated the editorial responsibility to a local attorney, Mr. A. Strong. These men printed a weekly newspaper, "The Kansas City Enterprise." This arrangement proved most unsatisfactory. The men committed found it took too much time from their other business interests.

While Mr. Payne was again in St. Louis on other business, he met a young man named Robert Thompson Van Horn. Mr. Van Horn was working on riverboats on the Ohio and the Mississippi Rivers. Mr. Van Horn had studied law, taught school, and worked as an editor on a newspaper in Ohio.

His associates gave Mr. Payne the power of attorney, and he offered to sell the "Enterprise" to Robert Van Horn for $500.00. No one foresaw the impact this bright young man would have in the growth of the small City of Kansas.

Van Horn made the trip to the western border of Missouri to investigate the offer Payne made. He was anxious to look the city over and talk with other people who held interest in the "Enterprise." Van Horn was evidently pleased with what he observed; they reached an immediate agreement. He paid $250.00 upon taking over the equipment with the balance due at the end of one year.

Van Horn took over and started operation of the newspaper. He did an excellent job, and in doing so identified himself with the community's hope and future. The gentlemen from whom he purchased the paper refused to take his money when it came due. They presented him a receipt for the full amount of his purchase.

That was the first of many examples Van Horn gave to show his initiative, enthusiasm, hard work, and love for the city. It built Kansas City into the large metropolis we know today. Van Horn seemed to have a gift few men possessed — insight into the future.

He was very much a gentleman of action, always working to make the city more prosperous and a better place to live. Van Horn extended extra effort to secure the charter of the Hannibal – St. Joseph Railroad that was to run from Cameron, Missouri. Later on, as a member of the U. S. Senate, he was most instrumental in gaining for the City of Kansas the site of the Hannibal Bridge (the first bridge constructed to span the Missouri River). Van Horn entered into a treaty with the Indians for the right to build a railroad across Indian Territory to Texas. The Missouri-Kansas Railroad soon reaped the fruits of that treaty.

In May 1861, he applied to General Lyon for state authority to enlist three hundred men in the State Militia to support the Union cause. General Lyon granted permission and gave him the commission of Major. His small army saw their first battle and victory in western Missouri on July 18, 1861. Van Horn was wounded in the first battle, which occurred at Lexington, Missouri. After his recovery, he was

Figure 43
Robert Thompson Van Horn
Photo: Hugh Chase Private Library

involved in many important battles, including Shiloh and Corinth. His valor in that battle earned the rank of Colonel.

Colonel Robert Van Horn was known as a man of accomplishments. Listing all his accomplishments would fill several books. The citizens held such respect for him that he won election to and held almost every elective office possible. He was Alderman, Mayor (three terms), Postmaster, a member of the State Senate and elected to the United States Senate in 1864, 1866, and 1868. Van Horn placed Abraham Lincoln in nomination in 1864.

Robert Thompson Van Horn was a man of wide vision and foresight that few men possess. Much of the growth that this city and the surrounding areas have enjoyed must credit his efforts and effectiveness. One of Robert T. Van Horn's descendents served out a career as a police officer on the Kansas City Missouri Police Department. He worked in the property room for several years. His name was Ralph Van Horn.

TOUGHEST BEAT IN TOWN

IN THE 1890's, someone wrote the following tribute to Kansas City's law enforcement officers: "The police force has long been known to be one of the very best in the country and a terror to evil-doers." Quite a statement, but the police blotter at the time seems to bear out the author's claim.

Kansas City was a vigorous young city fighting for growth

Figure 44 — Tough Beat, indeed!
Photo: Hugh Chase Private Library

and prominence. The city boasted a population of 200,000 and corporate city limits of more than fifteen square miles. Law enforcement within those boundaries was no easy task, but her 53 policemen, captained by L. E. Irwin, were up to the challenge.

Eight of those men were: Patrolmen Atkinson, Cooper, McNully, Prather, Keenan, West and Sergeants Dwyer and Wilson. They had a particularly difficult job. It was their responsibility to patrol the railroad yards of the Sheffield District, considered by some to be the toughest beat in Kansas City. Transients, many of whom were dodging the law, were a constant problem around the railroad yards. These men frequently resorted to violence to elude captivity.

Since those early days, Kansas City has seen changes in her Police Department. The uniforms are different. The equipment is vastly different; even the methods of fighting crime have been updated and improved. One important thing hasn't changed — the good people doing duty on the beat. Whether riding in a patrol car, on a motorcycle or patrolling on foot, they are still made of equal parts duty, loyalty, and pride mixed with a whole lot of courage. They will always be a vital asset to our community and its well-being.

Figure 45 — 1886 Election special officers
Hugh Chase Private Library

CAPTAIN MALLOY

The following interview was conducted and appeared in the "Kansas City Globe" printed February 10, 1890.

"A Policeman's Reminiscences"

Captain Malloy is one of the oldest policemen in the city and has passed through many exciting scenes during his experiences of nearly a quarter of a century. He recalls the time Jefferson Davis accepted an invitation to deliver an address at the Kansas City Fair Grounds. The intelligence that the leader of lost causes would speak upon the very border of Kansas aroused considerable excitement in that state, and it was rumored that Col. Jennison, at the head of three-hundred of his famous "Red Legs," would appear for the purpose of hanging Davis who was not a believer in Reconstruction. Captain Malloy was assigned as head of a special force of seventy-five officers to protect Mr. Davis. An immense crowd estimated at 50,000 people filed into the fair grounds, which was then located well down toward the center of the present city limits, near Troost Avenue. Captain Malloy deployed his men in double file extending from the gateway of the speakers stand. Mr. Davis, accompanied by Dr. Munford, at whose residence he was entertained while visiting in the city, reached the grounds safely. The precautions taken insured that no attempt was taken to disturb the speaker.

At one time during the afternoon a stranger from across

the state line attempted to create a tumult, but it was promptly squelched by a brawny policeman who picked him up by the waist. He was carried out bodily from the fair grounds. Mr. Davis remained only the one day.

Captain Malloy also reflected upon his memory of Cook's Pasture as a favorite resort for thieves and other bad characters about 1875. The pasture was also noted as a prime picnic area. It extended from Baltimore Avenue to the bluffs at Seventeenth Street. The pasture held a beautifully shaded grove. It also had a spring that always emitted clear cool fresh water. Many of the Indians and the Santa Fe traders quenched their thirst from this excellent source of drinking water. At times trouble would erupt between the Traders and the Indians. The police were frequently called to Cook's Pasture to quell these disturbances and restore peace and calm to the participants. The police were often assisted in these forays to the pasture by a big St. Bernard dog.

Speaking of dogs, Captain Malloy was reminded recently of a great mastiff named Bulger, property of Mayor Milton McGee, when McGee held the chair of Chief Magistrate in the growing metropolis of Kansas City. Bulger was the largest dog in town and a fighter of no little ability. He strutted about in a collar to which was attached a metal plate nearly twelve inches in diameter. It was inscribed in large letters, "TAX PAID."

One day the police were notified that a dogfight was in progress on the public square. Captain Malloy rushed to the scene to find that Bulger and a dog belonging to a butcher whose shop was in the public market square were fighting. Mayor McGee was the most interested spectator. He was leaning forward urging his dog on to victory. The Mayor was promptly arrested for instigating a dogfight. He was arraigned before police court and assessed a fine of ten dollars. Mayor McGee was noted for his generosity and was looked upon as one of the most popular men in the city.

TOM MORRISON

WHEN ONE RESEARCHES Kansas City Missouri Police Department history, one would surely look twice at stories of "Tom (Crack a Day) Morrison." In his colorful way, Tom Morrison and his family gave much to Kansas City citizens and the police department, adding to its proud heritage.

Thomas William Morrison was born January 7, 1866. He was the son of a Scottish cabinetmaker. His father died at sea in route to the United States. Tom grew up in Austin, Texas and came to Kansas City as a young man in 1885. Shortly after his arrival, the Kansas City and Westport Railway Company employed him. Mules powered the railway and Tom owned the mule; they hired both.

Eighteen hundred ninety-four was an election year in the city of Westport. Tom decided to seek the office of City Marshal. When the polls closed and the votes tabulated, Tom won over several opponents with votes to spare. The new marshal's domain extended from Twenty-First Street south to Forty-Seventh Street and from State Line east to Troost Avenue.

Tom served the city of Westport well, although his duties differed greatly from those of the more modern day police officer. Many citizens drove their horses and teams as far as Westport. They left their horses and rigs tied there and caught the more convenient streetcar into Kansas City. Marshal "Tom" considered it his duty to know which rig belonged to whom, and to see that the rigs headed in the right direction to reach home in safety.

Figure 46 — Kansas City, Missouri Police Department 1896
Hugh Chase Private Library

On December 2, 1897, the voters of Westport decided to become a part of Kansas City, Missouri. This meant that the office of the City Marshal of Westport ceased to exist, along with the town. Tom met the Chief of Police of Kansas City, John Hayes. The next day Tom Morrison started work for the Kansas City Missouri Police Department. He worked there fifty years, until retirement. He served as a sergeant at headquarters for many years. This is where he acquired his famous nickname, "Crack a Day." When Tom took part in planning a raid or making an important arrest, he always tried to carry it out at the crack of day. A few retired officers still recall Tom Morrison by that nickname.

During the latter part of his police career, he was assigned as beat officer to the Union Station. It was from here that many Kansas Citians remembered him. He was an officer who would go far beyond the patience of most men to assist a traveler having problems. His duty at the Union Station was also the most amusing of his police career.

Tom related this story often and always with a chuckle.

One morning he stood in the lobby looking over the arriving passengers, and someone tapped him on the shoulder. He turned to greet a woman holding a four-foot ape by the hand, as though he were a child. Tom was astonished. "Officer," asked the woman, "can you tell me where I can find a tree my ape can climb for his morning exercise?" Morrison recovered from his surprise enough to tell her she might find a tree in Washington Square. Off she went leading the ape by the hand with a curious crowd following on her heels. In Washington Square, the ape scampered up a tree, cavorted among the branches, and then accompanied his mistress back to the station. The animal then stood patiently while his mistress enjoyed a soft drink at the drug store soda fountain. In telling about it later, Morrison said, "Bar none, that was the strangest request ever made of me in all my years on the Police Department." That included the time he was

Figure 47 — Washington Square with view of Union Station, ca. 1930. *Photo: Kansas City Library Special Collection Photographs.*

Figure 48
Crowds at Union Station
Hugh Chase Private Library

Marshal at Westport.

"Crack a Day" Morrison spent many years apprehending many criminals at the Union Station. They thought catching a train into Kansas City assured their escape. They never figured on sharp-eyed Tom, who missed nothing in observing anyone who came through the lobby. Tom Morrison felt nothing but a tremendous sense of pride reserved for fathers when his son, Lawrence, followed in his footsteps and chose law enforcement as a career. This pride turned to a deep sorrow when his son died at Fifty-Ninth and Morningside Drive while in pursuit of a speeder. This occurred September 10, 1938, and the sorrow of this tragedy lingered for years.

Tom Morrison passed away on January 15, 1951 after serving as the last Marshal of Westport and fifty years as an outstanding police officer. Sergeant Richard Graff later carried out the family tradition of law enforcement. Sergeant Graff held the distinction of being the grandson of Thomas William "Crack a Day" Morrison.

Figure 49
Sergeant Richard Graff
Photo:
The Informant
December 1969

CHIEF JOHN HAYES

CHIEF JOHN HAYES served Kansas City as its fifth Chief of Police. He served from August 27, 1899 to 1906. He gained this most important position through long years of hard work and strict attention to duty. He carried out his job with great attention to detail. This enabled him to rise to the office of Chief of Police from a Texas freighter.

Chief Hayes was born in Rockford, Illinois. His parents migrated to Ottawa, Kansas when he was a small lad. In 1868, young John Hayes started working in the freight business. His job took him into Texas and the Indian Territory. He left the freight business and made his permanent home in Kansas City. He engaged in various pursuits before the Kansas City Missouri Police Department employed him.

John first worked as a patrolman in 1880. For nine years, he walked a beat under the supervision of Chief of Police Thomas M. Speers. He gained promotion from a beat patrolman to the rank of detective. In this position, his talents soon became noticed and he established a reputation of being one of the most competent "catchers of thieves" in the Middle West. After serving eight years as a detective, he advanced to the rank of inspector. In August 1897, the State Supreme Court ruled on Thomas Vallins' ineligibility for appointment as Chief of Police. They appointed Hayes acting Chief and a short time later named him permanent Chief of Police. He fulfilled this position with energy and credence.

Chief Hayes was a man who could go out "on the bricks"

at most any time and return with the lawbreaker he was seeking. The officers who worked for him swore his eyes never rested. They were constantly darting from one person to the other in an effort to ferret out the wrongdoers.

One day Hayes and Detective Charles Sanderson were walking on Main Street when two men appeared in the doorway of the Junction Building. Hayes and Sanderson spoke together for a moment then parted. "Those fellows are burglars." Hayes said to his partner. "You go after one and I'll get the other." Sanderson followed instructions and they arrested both men. They found a set of fine burglary tools on each suspect. His natural instinct as a detective told him to treat these men as suspects.

Chief Julian Snow once related a story about John Hayes. According to Chief Snow's account, Hayes was on a streetcar bound for home. He was passing Tracy Avenue when his eyes glimpsed three men standing in the shadows. These men looked suspicious to Hayes. Did he call for help or back up? No! He never gave such a thing a thought. Hayes knew he could arrest one or more men, desperate or otherwise, without bluster, blare of trumpets, or brandishing firearms. He required no help. He had a knack for timing his arrest at the crucial moment. He left the streetcar unnoticed by the men he had observed. He trailed the men to Belmont Flats at Fifteenth Street and Tracy Avenue. He bagged the three of them in the act of breaking and entering the building.

Chief Hayes was an outstanding police officer, physically toned, and loyal to the department and his fellow officers. Chief Hayes was a man of his word. The case of "Carey Snyder" shows the efforts Hayes took to keep his word.

The police arrested young Mr. Snyder, son of a wealthy banker, along with a well-known crook. They were charged with robbing a couple in their home at Twenty-Second and Troost Avenue, taking nearly five-thousand dollars worth of diamonds. Police recovered the diamonds in a Chicago pawnshop. They held the seasoned criminal but released Snyder on a personal bond in the custody of two well-known bankers. Snyder expressed his gratitude to Chief Hayes by leaving the city. Chief Hayes received public criticism for allowing Snyder's release and subsequent departure for parts unknown. Chief Hayes swore to himself, the victim, and the citizens that Snyder would be returned. He assigned two detectives to the case with implicit instructions to do nothing else but locate Snyder. He was holed up at a ranch fifty miles from Tulsa, Oklahoma, but before detectives could reach his hideaway to bring him to justice, he fled. After ten months searching for Snyder, he was found in Billings, Montana and brought back to Kansas City to stand trial. Chief Hayes spent $1,100.00 from his own pocket to bring Snyder to justice; John kept his word.

During his years as a policeman, John Hayes figured in many sensational arrests. At one time, a series of bold robberies terrified the city. The city was plagued with one or two hold-ups every evening. During this period, two men, one short and one tall, committed many of these robberies. They walked boldly into a shop while the proprietor counted his days' receipts, held up the victim, and calmly walked away. They always wore masks. The tall and the short suspects steadily grew bolder. This bothered Chief Hayes, and he decided to apprehend the culprits himself.

Captain Thomas Phillips, a city license inspector, Detective Patrick Cahill of the Kansas City Kansas Police Department, and Chief Hayes were searching the area of Tenth Street and Grand Avenue for a person named on an arrest warrant. Two men attracted Chief Hayes' attention as they walked down Grand Avenue. "There are the two robbers — the tall and the short man — looking in that store window," said Chief Hayes calmly. "Let's get 'em." When Chief Hayes said, "Let's get 'em," the others knew what he meant. Hayes collared the tall man whose name turned out to be Johnson. The others took charge of the short man whose name was Hatton. Both men put up a fight and both were heavily armed. They both received long penitentiary sentences after a guilty verdict at trial.

One time Hayes and two other officers went into a section of the city known as "Toad-a-Loup." It was a lawless section between the two Kansas Cities. They went to apprehend "Bill Burke," a notorious highwayman. This event took place in 1888. A desperate pistol duel ensued between Hayes and Burke. In the melee, Burke shot Hayes in the heel and escaped. Hayes swore vengeance, and he later arrested the highwayman.

When Chief Hayes left the Kansas City Missouri Police Department, he worked as a private detective for several years before his death. William Pinkerton, a well-known detective of his time, once said, "John Hayes was the shrewdest officer I have ever met. He was a detective by instinct. While other men depended on informants to solve cases, Chief Hayes used his power of intuition."

CARRIE NATION

IT WAS APRIL 15, 1901 when Mrs. Carrie Nation appeared in Kansas City. Mrs. Mary E. White accompanied her. Mrs. Nation was known as "The Joint Smasher" because of her "Hatchet Raids" in which she wrecked many saloons throughout the Midwest.

The ladies dropped into the saloon of Mr. M. A. Flynn, located at 117 East Twelfth Street, while on tour. They immediately took exception to the pictures decorating the walls of his establishment. "You would strip your own mother and hang her picture on these walls just to drag young men to Hell," Carrie shouted.

The bartender, Mr. Montville, attempted to calm her down. When he found he was unable to reason with her or quiet her down, he "bounced" her out the front door. Mr. Sparks, a city detective, happened along shortly after the bouncing incident. Mrs. Nation had gathered a crowd in the middle of Twelfth Street, and entertained them with one of her famous sermons on alcohol and its effects.

Detective Sparks tactfully and politely attempted to talk her into breaking it up and going her own way. Carrie had a crowd willing to listen and she was just getting warmed up; she wasn't about to let such an opportunity pass. She loudly refused to comply with the officer's request. He summoned the "hoodlum" wagon, placed Mrs. Nation and her companion inside, and transported them to the Central Police Station.

Figure 50
Carrie Nation
Photo:
Hugh Chase
Private Library

The station captain ordered them booked. They were placed in a cell where they remained until Carrie Nation's brother came to their rescue by posting a six-dollar bond. During their brief ride to the station and their incarceration, both ladies wept copiously.

The following morning the police court convened, with Carrie as the chief curiosity. She attracted more than three hundred people into the tiny courtroom. She sat to the right of Judge McAuley and attempted to recite verse after verse of scripture in his ear. During her case, Mrs. Nation questioned the officers who testified against her. After they related their side of the story, she started giving her account.

"Judge, these officers have lied. They are perjurers, malicious paupers, who receive pay for doing their duty and then fail to do it. Why don't they tear down those vile pictures on the wall of that saloon? Those pictures do more harm than I ever..."

"That will do out of you," interrupted the judge. "We are not interested in one of your sermons and we have no intention of listening to one in this court. I fine you five dollars or you have until six o'clock this evening to be out of the city." Judge McAuley quickly added, "Out of the state, too. Missouri is no place for you. This atmosphere does not agree with longhaired men or whistling women. I advise you to return to Kansas."

Carrie was temporarily speechless. For several minutes, the only comment she made was "Umph."

"I'm going to Liberty this afternoon," Mrs. Nation whispered after a moment of indignant silence. "That will necessitate my returning to Kansas City to return to my home in Kansas. Will that be all right?"

"Yes, if you don't start one of your sermons while you are here and cause us trouble," answered McAuley. "We are not about to have our community upset by someone like you when we can prevent it."

Mrs. Nation returned to the station to claim her case bond. A large crowd was waiting for her on the sidewalk when she returned. Chief Hayes requested that she depart by the City Hall entrance to avoid the mob of people gathered outside. She refused; she was anxious to meet the crowd. The "joint smasher" left the building after she presented Judge McAuley with a miniature hatchet as a souvenir of her visit to his court.

When Carrie arrived at the police station that morning, she espied one of the detectives smoking a cigar. "Do you know your smoking that thing offends me?" asked the smasher. "It makes me ill to smell a horrid cigar. If you only knew how vile a habit smoking is, you'd stop it, at least in my presence."

"If you would stay home in Kansas where you belong, wash your children's neck and ears, and keep your house clean you wouldn't be forced to smell this cigar," retorted the detective as he spun on his heel and walked away.

Mrs. Nation had turned to Mr. Hadley with a piece of paper in her hand. She displayed the address of Mr. Flynn's saloon on it. She softly remarked that she would like to sign a warrant for Mr. Flynn's arrest. The charge was violation of the Sunday closing ordinance. Mr. Hadley attempted to explain that this was a matter of regulation and the police had more than they could handle by apprehending burglars, murderers and other criminals.

1924 City Union Mission 1936

537-539 Main Street

Kansas City, Mo.

Down in the human heart,
Crushed by the tempter,
Feelings lie buried
that grace can restore:
Touched by a loving heart,
Wakened by kindness,
Chords that are broken
will vibrate once more.

TWELFTH ANNIVERSARY

CURRENT EXPENSE AND IMPROVEMENT CAMPAIGN

September 18th to 28th, 1936

THE ARM OF THE CHURCH — OPEN EVERY DAY AND NIGHT

He that giveth unto the poor shall not lack.—Proverbs 28:27

Figure 51 — Front Copy of Actual Report City Union Mission Twelfth Anniversary Current Expense and Improvement Campaign September 18 to 28, 1936

Carrie Nation was swelling with excitement. A tinge of red spread over Mr. Hadley's face. "You refuse then, to issue a warrant, do you?"

"I do," Mr. Hadley replied.

"You are just like the rest of them; you are a perjurer and wind break for the hell holes of Kansas City." As she spoke, her eyes lost their feline cunning and assumed a flash that always accompanied her smashing. While Mr. Hadley was trying to reason with her and give her an explanation, she stormed from the room shaking her fist at him and drowning out his argument with a din of verbal abuse. "You're rotten; you're rotten! And all the city officials are cut from the same cloth as you," she screamed as she stomped down the stairs.

Mr. Hadley fired after her that the people of Jackson County could very well solve their own problems without any assistance from her.

Carrie Nation held a very deep hatred for any alcoholic beverage and held contempt for those who sold it. Her first hatchet raid took place on a saloon in Wichita, Kansas. Many followed the first one. She always gave one of her lectures (sermons) any time she could find a listening ear. She was always ready to speak out about alcohol and its ill effect on society.

In February 1911, while giving one of her lectures in Arkansas, she suffered a stroke. She was taken to Leavenworth, Kansas, and she passed away on June 9, 1911. Carrie Nation was buried in the cemetery at Belton, Missouri, where a large monument stands in her memory.

Figure 52 — Sketch by Officer Bill Cronley
The Informant — September 1970

FIRST TRAFFIC ACCIDENT

THE FIRST ACCIDENT, involving the only two automobiles in Kansas City, happened in May 1901.

It was a bright and cheerful day sometime in early May. There was no hint of any great event. Two steamer cars, sputtering and emitting smoke approached Fifteenth Street and Oak. They met with a careening lurch a short way from the Christian Church; and so in 1901, the age of the crashes began.

How ironic that there were only two motor cars in Kansas City and they collided! They had the whole town to themselves. The streets and avenues were broad; there was no traffic congestion. There was a plentitude of pedestrians and horses (if something was hit), and yet they crashed into each other.

This momentous event on a bright May morning in 1901 took place on Fifteenth Street between Oak and Locust Streets. No monument marks the spot, but the crash's echoes reverberate almost hourly in every part of the city. About eleven o'clock that morning, Dr. A. H. Cordier breezed out of the Scarritt Hospital at Askew and Gladstone Boulevard, elated at the completion of a successful operation. He climbed into the driver's seat of the loco mobile steamer he purchased in March. He started toward the downtown district. His friend, Dr. Eugene Carbaugh, rode with him. They turned west at Fifteenth Street and sped along at twelve miles an hour, the old car steaming along beautifully. Horses shied along the side streets and teamsters cursed.

Why was Herbert A. (Bert) Wolpole traveling east on Fifteenth Street at the same instant, sitting proudly at the control lever of his steamer? The undiscerning explanation would be that he was going home to lunch. From today's perspective, he was a tool of fate. The crash age began right there.

Mr. Ray Oliver, horse fancier, rode in the automobile with Mr. Wolpole. He was in the lumber business. He sneered at the horseless carriage and required considerable persuasion to ride in such a contraption. As Mr. Wolpole crossed Oak Street and Dr. Cordier passed Locust, extra sensory perception seemed to take over. A mutual thought entered both their minds. Here is Doctor Cordier's own account of what took place. "I thought I would throw a scare into Bert and I guess Bert thought he would scare me. We veered toward each other. As we approached, we fully intended to swerve out of the way in plenty of time. I guess Bert lost control. Anyway, our cars bumped each other head on." This is quite possibly the birth of the alibi.

Mr. Wolpole stated, "I thought I would scare the Doctor, and I guess he thought he would scare me. We steered toward each other fully intending to turn out and miss each other at the last second. I guess the Doctor lost control and we bumped head-on."

The cars crashed as described. Dr. Carbaugh was thrown over the dashboard, his belt and trousers catching on the carbide light. He hung suspended there; head down, kicking frantically. They discovered Mr. Oliver in the street after the collision. It was long a debatable point whether he jumped or fell out. At any rate, his first words were, "I knew it all the time. I told you that damn thing would do it." The respective drivers kept their seats. A large crowd gathered to exchange "I told you so's." Several horse traders in the crowd extended their cards. The cars received no damage and proceeded to their destinations. The drivers parted friends and neither was ever involved in another collision.

From that incident so long ago, many firsts erupted. It was the first two car accident in the United States, the first alibi, (and because of that accident) the first known traffic law.

FIRST TRAFFIC FATALITY

AFTER SEEING so many automobile accidents and reading of the many lives taken by traffic fatalities each year, it makes one wonder when the first traffic death occurred in Kansas City. One would also note the circumstances surrounding the first traffic fatality. After proper research and investigation, we believe the following account might answer some of these questions.

Shortly before six o'clock p.m., October 27, 1906, R.M. Snyder, a capitalist, left his office at 316 American Bank Building to go to his home at 2806 Independence Boulevard. He stepped into his motor car, a 40 horsepower Royal Tourist. He spoke cheerfully to his chauffeur, "Rather late tonight Frank. Let's get along lively."

Mr. Snyder took his seat and relaxed directly behind his chauffeur. The chauffeur carefully guided the machine through the business streets of downtown from Admiral Boulevard to the junction with Grand Avenue. From that point on the speed increased and the big car glided smoothly along at a fast rate of speed. They first encountered trouble when they reached the streetcar tracks at Independence Boulevard and Woodland Avenue.

"That's a Royal Tourist," Mr. Loose said to a companion, H.C. Edwards of 3008 East Seventh Street, as the car sped past them. Neither of them recognized Mr. Snyder. After crossing the streetcar track, Mr. Snyder's chauffeur, Frank Schroeder, again stepped up to high-speed. The little twenty horsepower Stevens-Duryea driven by Mr. Loose came on behind, but the larger, more powerful machine rapidly increased the distance between them.

A little boy, pulling a small coaster wagon, was crossing Independence Boulevard. He did not see the rapidly approaching motor car. Mr. Snyder's chauffeur was horrified to see the little boy when they were within 100 feet of the intersection of Park Avenue and almost in front of Bonaventure Hotel.

The chauffeur veered the speeding machine sharply to the right with the hope he could get close enough to the curb to avoid hitting the boy. His effort was useless; the big motor car struck the boy and the wagon, tossing them high in the air, with the wheels on the right side of the vehicle grating along the curb. The sudden twisting and lurching of the car threw Mr. Snyder far over to the right side. Ten feet beyond where the boy was struck was a trolley pole. Mr. Snyder's head struck that trolley pole. The plush motor car came to a halt seventy-five feet farther beyond the front of a grocery store belonging to J.M. Fenney of 2312 Independence Boule-

Figure 53 — First motorized Police Department paddy wagon.
Photo: Hugh Chase Private Library

Figure 54 — Kansas City, Missouri Police Department's first car — Packard Model 18. *Photo: Hugh Chase Private Library.*

vard. Glancing backward over his shoulder the chauffeur saw Mr. Snyder sprawled in a heap on the floor of the vehicle. Several patrons in the Bonaventure Hotel, adjoining the accident, ran to the motor car. They saw Mr. Snyder lying unconscious, his head covered in blood.

Mr. Loose's machine had arrived at the scene by this time. Frank Schroeder, the chauffeur, Mr. Edwards, and Mr. Loose lifted Mr. Snyder from the car and saw he was badly injured. A quick examination of the big motor car revealed that it had practically no damage. Mr. Edwards held Mr. Snyder in his arms while the chauffeur turned the vehicle around. He drove full speed to Agnew Hospital at Sixth Street and Woodland Avenue. There Dr. A.H. Cordier and Dr. James A. Eldridge met the injured man. Examination revealed a badly crushed skull. He died within two minutes after his arrival at the hospital. In the meantime, someone picked the boy up and carried him into the drugstore of Haller and Beack in the Bonaventure Hotel Building. He was unconscious and

Figure 55 — unidentified Kansas City, Missouri police officers — 1906. *Hugh Chase Private Library.*

bleeding from both ears. No one at the scene could identify the boy.

A call was put in to the police department, and they responded by dispatching an ambulance and a surgeon. The men who picked the boy up were unaware of another injury. Dr. G.E. Smith, Dr. Louis Beck, and Dr. J.C. Reed attended the boy while waiting for an ambulance.

The police sent for Professor Charles B. Reynolds, principal of the Garfield School, in an effort to identify the boy. He arrived about the same time as the police ambulance with D. F. Wilhelm. Professor Reynolds told them he was not acquainted with the lad and was unable to identify him. A number of boys and girls were admitted to the drug store in an effort to establish his identity. "I know him. His name is Arthur," said a little girl. "He takes German lessons from Miss Andrews."

Someone picked the coaster wagon up from the street

where it landed after the accident. There was the name "Arthur Roddell," printed on the bottom of the wagon. The unconscious boy went by ambulance to Agnew Hospital before they learned that he lived at 2300 Minnie Avenue and summoned his parents. Dr. Cordier and other doctors examined the boy. They found a fracture at the base of the skull and bruises on the left thigh, the knee and ankle as well as internal injuries. He died at 10:45 that evening.

The first recorded fatality was a double one. Another point of interest is that Dr. Cordier, who gave emergency treatment to both victims, was also involved in the first traffic accident recorded in Kansas City.

"ADAM GOD" RIOT

IT WAS LATE in the afternoon of December 8, 1908, when Officer Dalbow was leaving Police Headquarters at Fourth and Main. He walked out of the arched door toward a group of men, women, and children. James Sharp, a bearded preacher who had given himself the title of Adam God, waited with his band of heavily armed followers.

James Sharp claimed that one evening years before, a huge comet cleaved the heavens over his farm. At that instant, he heard a voice commanding him to preach and spread the word of God. Preach he did! When the spirit moved him in 1905, he and his band of followers paraded the streets of Oklahoma City as naked as Adam and Eve. In the winter of 1908, they floated from the north down the Missouri River on a houseboat. They tied up at the riverfront, planning to make Kansas City one of their stops on a great preaching tour down the river.

After their arrival, they found themselves in trouble over the children in the party. Sharp insisted the children in his group sing in the streets. This led to a tragedy that would take place on the paved street at Fourth and Main Streets. In later years, a witness put in writing what he remembered of that day.

When Officer Dalbow approached the group, he had said to Sharp, "The sergeant would like to see you." The group questioned him and asked if he came in peace. He replied in the affirmative. Sharp then put away his revolver and extended his right hand. At almost the same instant, a police photographer named Mullane stepped up behind Dalbow. He pushed a revolver over his shoulder and shouted at Sharp, "Drop that knife; drop that gun."

"Damn that sergeant," exclaimed Elmo Pratt (a member of Adam God's band). "I'm going to shoot that Sergeant." Another witness, who was racing to the Hannibal Bridge depot to catch a four o'clock train, stated he saw smoke spew up from the slanting gun held by Pratt. He also stated he observed a woman and a girl chase officer Mullane around a wagon, attempting to gun him down. The witness estimated thirty or forty shots fired in a period of six or eight minutes. When the smoke cleared and quiet settled over the street, several lifeless bodies lay on the pavement. Killed were Officers Mullane and Dalbow, Pratt and his daughter Lulu. An innocent bystander received a hand wound. Adam God had fled. A farmer who routed him out of a straw stack with a pitchfork near Olathe, Kansas captured him a few days later.

Sharp wept when told who had been killed. He had received a hand wound in the gunfight, and it was still bleeding. Adam God stated that he believed it was impossible for him to be shot because God was with him. He also told officers that his faith was shaken when a police bullet had grazed his hand.

The trial was held in May of 1909 in a court within a few blocks from the scene of tragedy. When asked the reason for arming himself, Adam God replied, "I was blind. The Lord left me blind to do evil. Jesus said to love your enemies. If I had known then what the Lord told me last night about my enemies being my friends, I would never have picked up those guns."

On May 29, 1909, the jury found Adam God guilty of second-degree murder and sent him to twenty years of reflection in the State Penitentiary.

STROLL

THE FOLLOWING is a suggestion for a pleasant stroll in the Kansas City Red Book (guidebook) in August of 1910. This stroll was intended for people who were passing through

Figure 56 — Points of interest on "The Stroll"
The Informant — November 1970

the city and found themselves with time on their hands while waiting for a train. They were to start from the Old Union Depot located between Ninth and Tenth Streets on Union Avenue. The guidebook directed them as follows:

We will assume that the visitor is a fair pedestrian and wishes to see as much of the city in as short of time as possible, and that his starting point will be the Union Depot, which was built and completed in 1877 at the cost of $410,000.00 and was used by eighteen railroads. You are directed to follow the street car tracks west until the state line is reached, then, if an inspection of the meat packing industry is desired, the Armour Packing Company officials are very obliging and will send guides through the house with visitors. From there walk up Central Avenue, east on James Street, crossing the viaduct and reaching the stockyards, where the stroll takes you up the Twelfth Street incline, giving a fine view of Kansas City's railroad industry. At Washington Street, turn aside to Thirteenth and view the beautiful Normal Build-

Figure 57 — Twelfth Street looking west
Hugh Chase Private Library

Figure 58 — Union Depot, ca. 1880
Photo: Kansas City Library Photographs

ing of Grace Episcopal Church. At Thirteenth and Central is the Convention Hall, the largest of its kind in the world, of Italian Renaissance style. It was here William J. Bryan was nominated and the famous Kansas City Platform was adopted.

At Eleventh and Broadway is the Roman Catholic Cathedral of the Immaculate Conception, with the Christian Brother's school. Also St. Theresa's Academy, from here it is but a short step to St. Joseph's Hospital, which commands a splendid view of the Missouri River Valley, and Nettleton home for the aged. Now, continue north on Fifth Street. Walk on Fifth Street to Main Street. Here is the City Hall, a fine structure. Building was begun in 1890 and completed in 1893 at a cost of $300,000.00. On the west side is a memorial to heroic policemen who died at their post of duty.

East is the City Market, for the sale of produce and fruits. Walk up Walnut Street to Missouri Avenue, then continue *along Missouri Avenue where you come to the County Courthouse, built of Warrensburg sandstone at a cost of $500,000.00, which resembles a beautiful old French chateau; from there follow the golden dome of the Post Office and Custom House, which was finished in 1900, and has already grown too small for the City's business. A trip to the summit will well repay the traveler; then walk up to Ninth and Locust Street to where the public library is located, a beautiful construction of Texas granite and Carthage limestone. The basement contains a fine museum. Upstairs is the Nelson Art Gallery.*

Continue east along Ninth, you enter the Paseo, walk south on Paseo to Fifteenth, then back to Twelfth. Take a street car on Twelfth Street west, get off at Main Street and walk north to Seventh Street, then go east to Walnut and up Walnut to Thirteenth. After window-shopping, the visitor is ready to return to the Depot to continue his journey by train.

CHIEF THOMAS P. FLAHIVE

THOMAS P. FLAHIVE was appointed Chief of Police of the Kansas City Missouri Police Department on May 4, 1917. Chief Flahive was a veteran member of the Police Department when he took the office of Chief. He gave the department thirty-six years of service within the Department and at the end, the Governor appointed him Chief. Many Boards of Police Commissioners had considered naming Thomas P. Flahive to head the Kansas City Police Department as Chief before he succeeded H. W. Hammil. Flahive's long spotless record with the department naturally suggested such action, but political maneuvers invariably resulted in other selections. This was a time when the city was in the midst of political machinations of shifting alignment, when factionalists held police jobs no more highly ethical than so many poker chips. It was a period when corruption, if not "open," was at least within whispering distance of the police. However, Tom Flahive kept himself clean and above suspicion.

Chief Flahive's appointment, after waiting thirty-five years, came at a time of declining health. The strain of this position could have been a contributing cause of his death. Workers called a streetcar strike shortly after Chief Flahive took office. The company misinformed the Police Department of their intentions. The street railway owners imported two trainloads of professional strikebreakers, and the "anti-fink" (anti-strikebreaker) riots that followed held the city in a perilous situation. Flahive's tact and coolness helped the besieged strikebreakers out of the car barns when stormed, and saw them safely out of town.

Chief Flahive was a hardworking, trustworthy police officer. Intelligent, but not a brilliant detective, he never grandstanded. "I'm a policeman. I obey orders," he often said. As an obedient soldier, he had to issue and carry out some distasteful commands. He never did this with any political ambition.

Flahive's pursued course as a policeman failed to win him the Chief's office, but he always brought undiminished vitality to the task. He won such public respect that an attempted expulsion from his office after the Hayes' "investigation" in 1900 was abandoned. Many remembered that Flahive had the courage to tell J.A. Reed, the Mayor, and R. L. Gregory, Police Commissioner, he "would not perjure himself for any man on the job." The Board, threatened with such a political storm, finally decided to drop any action against Flahive. These allegations concerned gambling protection during the Democratic National Convention held that year.

Chief Tom Flahive was born in Bally Heague, Kerry County, Ireland on December 16, 1861. He came to Kansas City at the age of sixteen. He was appointed to the Kansas City Police Department on June 12, 1881. Appropriately, Chief Flahive died while in office on June 26, 1918, after being critically ill for several weeks.

POLICE MONUMENT

THE POLICE MONUMENT stands at 1125 Locust Street. It was moved from Fifty-Eighth and The Paseo to its present location and re-dedicated on September 7, 1973. Prior to that, the Monument stood at Truman Road and The Paseo. Hugh Chase wrote the following in May of 1971 under his byline of the Kansas City Missouri Police Department's "The Informant" magazine.

"This location is where too few of our officers gather once

Figure 59 — Police Memorial Monument at 59th and Paseo Now located at 1125 Locust
Photo: Hugh Chase Private Library

a year and pay our respects to fellow officers, who gave their lives to living up to the oath that we are all expected to uphold as police officers. This writer feels that this monument is not only a tribute to these officers who gave their lives to their fellow citizens, but stands as a reminder to every Kansas City Police Officer who takes the oath that we, as peace officers, mean to ourselves and the community in which we serve. **Spotlight on History** *will cover some of the work that went into the erection of this monument with the hope it will take on a new meaning to the officers so that they and their families will take the one hour asked on May 30th to pay proper respect to our fellow officers, who have given their lives to our community."*

THE POLICE MEMORIAL MONUMENT

This monument is a nine-foot bronze statue placed on a red granite base. The base is approximately ten feet tall, making an overall height of nineteen feet. The monument has the names of officers who gave their lives in the discharge of their duties. The first name is Martin Hynes, 1881. The statue is one of the outstanding police statues in the United States today. The idea the sculptor wished to convey in 1920 is just as obvious today and will continue to be for hundreds of years to come.

The statue portrays a stalwart, long-coated law officer with a nightstick in his right hand, and a child resting in his left arm. The tiny head is snuggled against his shoulder with the unquestioning confidence of a youngster who has been rescued from a bad situation.

HISTORY OF THE MONUMENT

Officer William E. Bondurant was walking his beat on Grand Avenue and Walnut Street between Sixth and Twelfth Streets on a summer day in 1919 when Mr. W.E. Kemper met him on the sidewalk near Commerce Trust Company and asked him to come into his office. Officer Bondurant went in with him and Mr. Kemper said, "Officer, I'm getting tired of that old police statue in front of the City Hall, and I would like for you to help me raise the money for a new police memorial." Every businessman along Officer Bondurant's beat contributed to the fund. Mr. Kemper met him a few days later and inquired if he would be as good at modeling as he was raising money. In order that the monument would not be a personal portrait statue, but a symbol of the police service, two men were selected by the committee headed by Mr. Kemper to pose for it. Officer Bondurant, who had taken an active part in the campaign to secure the memorial and whose features were well suited for the part, posed for the head. Officer Ira Boyle was selected to pose for the figure. Three different children posed for the child's figure, which is also a composite. They were Donald Patterson, Miss Marjorie Bondurant, and Miss Margaret J. Boyle. The five people who posed for the statue spent eight to nine hours a day working with the sculptor in a garage at 3701 Troost for several months. Officer Bondurant was a member of the Kansas City Police Department from 1914 to 1923. Officer Ira Boyle was a member of the Kansas City Police Department from 1912 to 1926.

THE SCULPTOR

Robert Merrill Gage was born in Topeka, Kansas on December 26, 1892. He graduated from Topeka High School; following that, he went to New York City and studied the art of sculpturing under Gutzon Borglum, one of America's greatest sculptors. Mr. Borglum never took more than two or three students at a time, indicating Mr. Gage's talent.

Most notable of Gage's work was a bronze of Abraham Lincoln. He gave this work the title "The Man of Sorrows." He modeled this in the rear of a barn at 1031 Filmore Street, Topeka. A committee from the Kansas Congress went to the barn to view the model, with the intention of having this "kid" finish it for the state. They went to scoff but came away in praise. After many months of work on this model and after viewing over one hundred pictures of Lincoln before its completion, the monument was unveiled and still stands in front of the Kansas State House. Borglum, his first teacher, came from New York to attend the unveiling of this monument. He said, "Gage is America's most promising young sculptor." Among other monuments to his credit are:

- "Mother and Child"
- "Father Love"
- "Mother Love"
- "John Brown"
- "The Eternal Idol"
- Figures of Agriculture and Industry — State Building, California.
- Sculpture on "Edison Building" — Los Angeles, California.
- Sculpture on "Outdoor Theater" — Redlands, California.
- Sculpture of Fountain at Beverly Hills, California.

Mr. Gage was a member of Washburn University Faculty in Topeka. He also lived in Kansas City at 3701 Troost in 1916, and had a class of art students in the Kansas City Fine Arts Institute. He was a winner of the Gold Medal from the Kansas City Art Institute in 1921, and a winner of the Gold Medal at the Pacific Southwest Exposition. Gage served many years as Assistant Professor of Sculpture at the University of Southern California.

FIRST TRAFFIC SIGNAL

PRIOR TO 1921, Kansas City had no traffic signals. Control of vehicular movements rested solely in the hands of a small group of police officers assigned to motorcycles and specific intersections within the central business district.

On January 8, 1921, the director of the Kansas City Council requested permission from the Park Department to erect a semaphore. This stood on a six-foot square platform two feet high in the intersection of Linwood and Paseo. The Park

Figure 60 — Early Police Patrol automobile
Hugh Chase Private Library

Figure 61 — Early Police Department automobile (in front of Police Station No. 3). *Hugh Chase Private Library*

Board granted this request, and the semaphore was installed and put into operation on January 23, 1921.

On July 9, 1922, a temporary circular wooden fence one and one half foot high and fifty feet in diameter was built in the center of this intersection. A police officer stationed inside this enclosure, with a member of the Safety Council, instructed motorists. On September 5, 1922, the director of Kansas City Safety Council arranged for the placement of a "silent policeman" for safety at Twentieth and McGee. This was a long narrow sign on an iron pedestal, which carried the words "Go To The Right." A red flag stayed on the top during daylight hours and a red light at night. This device kept motorists from cutting the corner when making a left turn.

On October 16, 1922, the Automobile Club installed a stop signal at Twenty-sixth and Penn. This was the only signal light in the city at that time. *The Kansas City Star* carried a story to the effect that a four-way signal would be installed at Eighteenth and McGee. This occurred May 24. The article stated the four-way suspended signal went into operation at Linwood and Troost. The Kansas City Power and Light Company installed the signal. It functioned automatically at thirty-second intervals at the cost of $750.00 per year.

The lights operated daily from 6:00 a.m. until midnight. A bell rang during the amber cycle. To further facilitate the movement of traffic, a centerline was painted on McGee from Fifteenth Street (Truman Road) to Twentieth Street, with stop lines at the intersections.

On September 7, 1924, overhead-suspended signals were activated in Kansas City, Kansas on Minnesota Avenue at the intersections of Fifth, Sixth, and Seventh Streets. Horizontal signals were activated on the four corners of the intersections of Sixteenth, Seventeenth, Eighteenth, Twentieth, and McGee in Kansas City, Missouri.

On September 24, 1924, Police began the use of hand-operated semaphores at Twelfth and Grand Avenue, Twelfth and Walnut, Twelfth and Main, Twelfth and Baltimore, Elev-

Figure 62 — 1920's Unidentified motorcycle officer
Hugh Chase Private Library

Figure 63 — 1920's Unidentified motorcycle officers
Hugh Chase Private Library

Figure 64 — 1920's Motorcycle Officer Bledsoe
Hugh Chase Private Library

enth and Grand, and Eleventh and Walnut. During 1925, more signals were installed at strategic locations. A four-way signal was put into operation at Linwood and Paseo on October 3, 1927, and the amber cycle after green was for left turn movement only.

Today, we have approximately six hundred sixty-seven signals in operation in Kansas City. In 2002, there were five million automobiles traveling the streets of Kansas City, Missouri.

HORSES

ON SEPTEMBER 24, 1924, the sight of a riderless horse walking down Grand Avenue amid traffic (in the heart of downtown) shocked any stranger to Kansas City. That stranger might be tempted to watch for a moment, and then follow in pursuit.

Sergeant W.H. Arnold, in charge of the Police Department's Mounted Traffic Squad, selected that day to

Figure 65 — Lonnie Quick and his horse Teddy
Photo: The Informant, July 1969

allow his horse, Bessie, to perform. He gave Bessie a signal to follow at a distance. She caught the signal, and follow she did! Nonchalantly, Bessie passed through the vehicles as if they were fence posts and she was in a pasture. She obeyed so well that she was on the sidewalk as her trainer entered a store. Her trainer then informed her that such commands ended at the curbside.

Emulating Sergeant Arnold, the other members assigned to the traffic squad adopted the "Mary and her little lamb" idea. Most of the mounts learned to follow without the officer clucking or tempting them with sugar lumps. Some maintained several motorcar lengths, while others insisted they stay with their nose at their master's shoulder.

Kansas Citians gave a cordial welcome to the mounted traffic force. Mounted horsemen patrolling the congested area? Why? It was almost too good to be true. In the on-rush of modern progress, it seemed the horse was destined only for the bridle paths and wide open spaces beyond the city

Figure 66 — Various officers and their mounts
Photo: Hugh Chase Private Library

limits. The name "old Dobbin" appeared to suffice and generalize the whole situation. Now the horse returned. He moved right through the heart of motordom.

The fourteen-member traffic squad lined up ready for duty in the morning on Campbell and Fifteenth (Truman Road) Streets. Police Captain John E. Wilson authorized the formation and organization of the unit along with the selection and purchase of mounts. The squad started training in June 1924, and deployed that year during the Shrine convention.

Sergeant Arnold dwelled on his satisfaction thus: "All that is required of the officer is to make his way down the street, the traffic will move right along with the horse and rider. The horse will do the work. A policeman stationed in one spot can yell his lungs out and still be ignored. We have been able to keep the alleys clear and clean because we are able to move where before it was impossible. Also, any person in need of an officer can easily spot him from a distance."

If one discounted the practical aspect, they found the citizens of Kansas City delighted at the sight of the prancing bay horses, parading down the busy city streets.

They liked the resonant sound of hoof beats, and the sight of a mounted policeman giving polite reminders to parking violators.

The Barton Teaming Company at 1509 Campbell Street quartered the horses. It cost $32.00 a month for boarding each animal. Veterinary bills and shoe repairs cost an average additional fee of $6.00 per animal each month. Each animal needed shoes every five to six weeks. E.M. Donaldson, a gentleman who boasted that he learned to ride horses before he could walk, styled himself as the "boarding horse keeper." He always referred to the stables as the "barracks."

The squad had been set at fifteen horses with fourteen already obtained. Most were bay color, although a few of them were dark brown. They accepted no blacks or sorrels. All mounts were to be uniform in size and color. Each horse cost between $150.00 and $250.00. All were three- or five-gaited.

They were small, averaging 1,150 pounds in weight, and none measuring more than 15-1/2 hands high. Each officer named his own mount. This resulted in such names as Billy, Babe, Bessie, Bud, Pauncho and Prince.

A small paved yard sat in front of the stable. Here the officers, in their leisure hours, conducted an informal training school. One found Officer Frank Harlan teaching Prince to shake hands with his hoof or to paw the ground when asked his age. In the opposite corner of the yard, Rex learned to stand upright on his hind legs.

The stable boys had been contracted, but no one had figured on the personal interest and ambition of the officers regarding their mounts. Every officer displayed possessive pride in his animal and very particular ideas about their care and grooming. Each insisted they participate or give the task close supervision. Each officer looked at these tasks with interest and accepted full responsibility for their

Figure 67 — Downtown Kansas City as it might have appeared during reign of horses.
Photo: Hugh Chase Private Library

Figure 68 — 1928 Metropolitan Commanding Officers
Hugh Chase Private Library

animal's comfort. This seemed more an interesting hobby than part of their job. They reported at 9:00 a.m. to polish saddles and bridles. Roll call came thirty minutes later, then

Figure 69
Chief William A. Shreeve
Hugh Chase Private Library

off to their respective beats. They worked the street for eight hours with a one and a half hour break for lunch.

The men assigned to mounted detail were carefully selected and hand picked. The selection process depended on competition and experience. It was common knowledge that the horses were much smarter than many men were. This paid off in many ways. The men and animals selected gave Kansas City many hours of outstanding work. In a short time, they functioned as a crack drill team second to none in stiff competition.

The Police Department used the horses until 1929. Their final appearance as a unit came in a parade that year. They disbanded soon after that and the horses sold at an auction held on East Third Street.

POLICEWOMEN

IN THE YEARS 1968 and 1969, the Kansas City Police Department reorganized and hired the first women as a beginning to what is now the "modern policewoman." However, it was not a new idea to Kansas City. The Kansas City Police Department appointed the first policewoman of record on October 29, 1924. Those first ladies were appointed by Chief Shreeve when he announced he was drafting four matrons and two clerks to make up for a shortage of patrolmen needed on election day to fill in duties at election precincts. These

Figure 70
Rosie Mason
(One of first two women officers)
The Informant
December 1967

women had the same powers of arrest as the male police officers. If desired, they were permitted to arm themselves with a revolver.

Women were again appointed as patrolwomen May 18, 1929. They remained separated from the male officers with Mrs. Francis Trowbridge appointed as Chief of Women Police. Her office was in the Fire Station Building at Fifth and Main Streets. Mrs. Trowbridge spent several weeks studying the use of policewomen in St. Louis, Missouri before returning to Kansas City to put her plans and new ideas into action.

Mrs. Trowbridge made it clear that husbands who abandoned their wives or children and refused to support them would find it rough going. The policewomen tailed them relentlessly, intent on seeing justice done from a woman's standpoint. The women also investigated liquor or other criminal abuse. They carried no weapons nor did they have a badge in their purse. They merely obtained the evidence and turned it over to the men. Mrs. Trowbridge was of the

Figure 71
Carolyn Pate
(One of first two women officers)
The Informant
December 1967

opinion that women would talk to her women much quicker because women have a better understanding of each other. She pointed out that her policewomen were not social workers and all cases requiring social work were turned over to the proper agencies.

The Youth and Women's Division was put into effect on May 16, 1967 with the appointment of Rose Mason and Carolyn Pate to the Department as probationary patrolwomen. Three more young women were added August 1, 1967, with the appointments of Marylyn Stovall, Susan Castle and Kay Fuhrman. These young women were issued weapons and carried the same power of arrest as the male members of the department. These early policewomen maintained a full workload, with their assignments including shoplifting detail and special surveillance assignments. They filled many speaking assignments concerning public safety matters. They lectured and taught self-defense to lady's organizations. They handled investigations involving juveniles — no matter what the crime committed by the juvenile or committed upon them. The status of female officers remained the same until the mid-1970's. During the 1970's to date, the field of law enforcement changed for the female officer. She now goes through the same training as her male counterpart and assignment to the same work, whether it is patrol or investigation. The gender of the employee in law enforcement makes no difference as to where assigned. In 1968, the female officers' badge stated Patrolwoman and the male officers' badge stated Patrolman; today both state "Police Officer."

CHARLES H. (BERT) HENDERSON

MANY TIMES a police officer must execute a minor deed or service for a citizen. When the officer completes his call and is ready to return to service, the people whom he served might reward him with a thank you, a handshake, or a smile. This is the citizen's way, many times, of telling the officer how deeply they appreciate the officer's concern and willingness to assist them.

The following is a true story of a gentleman who had a silent and most unusual way of showing and expressing his feelings of gratitude to all members of the Kansas City, Missouri Police Department.

The year was 1927. Mr. Charles H. (Bert) Henderson resided at 533 Gladstone Boulevard. He worked as a clerk and bookkeeper at a local milling company in Kansas City. Mr. Henderson was much like any other hardworking citizen of his day, with one exception. He expressed his citizenship in a very quiet and unusual manner. This he accomplished by placing a special marker on the graves of Kansas City Police Officers.

Several years before anyone became aware of what he was doing, Mr. Henderson passed along "The Paseo" on Decoration Day. As he traveled south, near Fifteenth Street (Truman Road) and the Paseo, his attention focused on the Police Monument. He suddenly realized that there were no flags or decorations to honor the men it stood for. To Mr. Henderson, this seemed neither right nor proper. This is a holiday which we set aside to honor our dead, especially unsung, heroes. Yet officers who had given their lives to this city seemed forgotten.

As these thoughts passed through his mind, he recalled many incidents of bravery by many officers. He witnessed this in his youth while spending many happy hours visiting the police station. He remembered being in the company of some of the officers who walked a beat. It must have been during a moment with those thoughts that Mr. Henderson resolved to do his part toward commemorating the memory of the men on the Department.

Mr. Henderson soon designed and placed markers on the graves of Kansas City Police Officers. They were manufactured of metal and colored red, white, and blue. The letters "K.C.P.D." were boldly engraved on these markers. When he found or heard where an officer was buried, he placed a metal marker on the grave. He took great time and effort to locate

Figure 72
Police Memorial at Truman and Paseo
Now located at 1125 Locust
Photo: Hugh Chase Private Library

each grave. Mr. Henderson took flags and wreaths to decorate the graves of officers for more than five years before Department officials became aware of his one-man campaign.

After learning of his devotion, they summoned him to meet with them and explain his purpose. They learned that he financed this campaign strictly from his own pocket. When Mr. Henderson appeared before the Board of Police Commissioners, he related how many markers he had made thus far. He also told them the plans he hoped to carry out the following Decoration Day. Up to that date, he had marked 125 graves of policemen in Kansas City cemeteries and had records of officers' deaths dating back to 1882. In addition to these, Mr. Henderson located and marked graves of officers in eighteen other cities and towns. He also marked these with his special markers. Mr. Henderson also placed wreaths on both police monuments. One originally stood at Fifteenth and Paseo and now stands in front of Police Headquarters. The other stood beside the old City Hall.

The Commissioners, after meeting with Mr. Henderson, informed him that they would continue marking the graves in the future. They thanked him for pointing out how they could assist his program. Mr. Henderson provided flags and markers for the following year. Mr. Henderson was the son of Chief Alex Henderson, a member of the Kansas City Fire Department.

THE DETECTIVE ACE

ON DECEMBER 2, 1929 at 8:00 a.m., Homicide Detective Bert Haycock exited his home and entered his 1928 Nash Coupe, backed out of his driveway, and started south bound on the Paseo Boulevard. Detective Haycock was thinking about the lineup that he was to conduct at the Headquarters Building. He was just south of Sixty-First Street when a small closed car passed him going north. At Sixty-First Street, the car ahead slowed sufficiently to attract Detective Haycock's attention. He noticed there was no glass in

Figure 73
Chief Lincoln R. Toyne
Photo: Hugh Chase Private Library

the rear window. Then the barrels of two shotguns appeared. Detective Haycock realized these gangsters were attempting to shoot at him. He dropped to the floor of his vehicle just as both shotguns were discharged towards him. Haycock pulled on the emergency brake from his cramped position as two more shots crashed into the front of the car. After a slight delay, he peered through the windshield. The car from which the shots were fired had disappeared.

Haycock went to the nearest telephone and called the Country Club Police Station. He left his car standing in The Paseo. The windshield was unbroken. The chief damage to his car was in the puncturing of the vacuum tank. Twenty separate bullet holes were found in the radiator, the hood, and the cowl; but none of them had done serious damage. Detective Haycock was uninjured. All the shots had been fired too low, and he had been protected by the motor. Other motor cars were passing when the attack was made. There was a Marlborough Street Car, loaded with passengers, standing nearby taking on patrons. There was not a pause in the traffic due to the attempt on Detective Haycock.

The detective believed the attack might have been due to his investigation and arrest of persons suspected in the Sears-Roebuck robbery earlier in the year. He arrested four top gangsters in the crime syndicate of Kansas City.

In 1928, Detective Haycock was shot in both arms at Twenty-First Street and Grand Avenue by a bandit gang believed to have been led by Gus Nichols, notorious bank bandit. He was attempting to arrest Nichols and others following the hold-up of a police officer posing as a jewelry salesman.

Detective Haycock has been with the Police Department for many years, and was considered by Lincoln R. Toyne, former Police Chief, as an outstanding officer. He has made many arrests that might have furnished the motive for the attempt on his life.

E.P. Boyle, Chief of Detectives, accepted the attempt on Detective Haycock as a challenge to his Department, and instructed all the detectives to "oil up their shotguns." "Bring in the crooks," Chief Boyle instructed. "Visit their hide-outs and round them up. Somewhere you may get a tip that will lead to them."

Chief Boyle recalled the recent kidnapping of Officer E.E. Willcut, who was taken on a tour of bank and store robberies[1] by two bandits and then tossed out of a moving vehicle. "These crooks are becoming so bold they are sure to up their hands," the Chief said. "If the attempted assassination of Detective Bert Haycock is a result of his efforts in the Sears-Roebuck case, it may not stop there. Attempts may be made on the lives of other Detectives."

The shooters were never identified and are still unknown to this day.

1 *The Kansas City Times*, December 2, 1929

C.H. DINGMAN, JR.

LATE IN THE EVENING of December 2, 1929, three men entered the drugstore on the northwest corner of Twenty-Fifth Street and Brooklyn Avenue. John Watson, Joe Hershon, and Charles Curtis were ex-convicts recently released from the Missouri State Penitentiary in Jefferson City. After the three men entered the store, they milled around as if shopping until all customers had left the store. This left the storeowner, Estil Cashion, alone in the back of the store. At this time, two of them hurried toward Mr. Cashion. The third man kept to the front of the store where he watched the door and the street. Mr. Cashion glanced up and realized that he could not prevent the robbery. To take action to foil it could mean suicide. All he could do was obey their demands.

The first of the hold-up men forced him to lie on the floor face down while he bound Mr. Cashion hand and foot. The other bandit in the rear of the store quickly removed the money from the cash drawer. The three bandits left the drugstore with the sum of eighteen dollars. Before the evening ended, they paid a high price for this small sum of money.

Motorcycle patrolmen C.C. Coffeen, D.P. Glenn, and Charles H. Dingman, Jr. had been assigned to do their tour of duty in a patrol car due to the slick condition of the streets. The ice made the streets so slippery it was dangerous to use the "wheels," (as motorcycle officers refer to their cycles). The three officers cruised and checked the streets in the neighborhood near Thirty-First Street and Jackson Avenue.

Figure 74 — First three motorcycle officers, Kansas City, Missouri Police Department. (Middle officer, Edward L. Martin, other officers unknown) *Photo: Hugh Chase Private Library.*

A Ford car passing slowly in front of Hobbs and Skiles Drugstore, located on the northwest corner of Thirty-First and Jackson Avenue, drew their attention. The occupants of the Ford broke no law, but the manner in which they crept along eyeing the store gave the officers reason enough to check the car and occupants, run a check, and ask a few questions.

The officers touched the siren and hit the red light to signal the Ford to pull over. Officer Dingman left the patrol car and started toward the Ford. The occupants opened fire on Officer Dingman. Although seriously wounded, Dingman attempted to arrest these gangsters. He reached for the car, grabbing the handle of the right front door. They quickly ground the car into gear and sped away. The other two officers immediately returned fire. The suspects again stopped the get-away car to flee on foot. One ran east toward Spruce Avenue; the second ran across the street into a driveway. The third suspect fled across a vacant lot just north of 4037 Jackson. Coffeen gave chase to the one running into the driveway. They exchanged shots before the officer lost him in the darkness. Glenn pursued the third suspect who ran into a field. He also lost his man in the darkness.

Losing sight of the fleeing suspects, the two officers turned their attention to Officer Dingman. He returned to the patrol car before collapsing in the street. Aided by Mr. Edward McNeese of 3027 Jackson Avenue and other neighborhood citizens, the officers carried Dingman into the McNeese home. The officers, with the help of Mr. and Mrs. McNeese, administered first aid to the wounded officer until he went to St. Luke's Hospital by ambulance. Upon arrival, the young officer succumbed to his injuries and died.

When other officers arrived at the scene, one of them telephoned the license number from the bandits' car into the auto theft unit. A.H. Jackson made the check at once against the book of state motor vehicle registrations. The check revealed a license issued to a Ford motor car owned by a drive-it-yourself car rental company located at 3037 Prospect.

Police Detectives Haycock, Stewart and Rayon rushed to the car rental company. While they questioned the manager of the rental company, they discovered that the gangsters made a big mistake. One of the gunmen gave the rental company his correct name and address. There on the rental application appeared the name John Watson, 3034 Walnut Street.

Detective Haycock, still somewhat "hot" from an attempt made on his life the night before, carried a sawed-off shotgun and a revolver. He urged the others to hurry. They loaded into the police vehicle and sped to the Walnut Street address.

The three Detectives stationed themselves inside the house out of sight after ascertaining that no one was home. They waited until they heard the footsteps of two of the gangsters climb the stairs. The two gangsters were Watson and his cohort Hershon, both involved in the robbery and the shooting of the Police Officer. They walked unsuspectingly into the room where the detectives waited to make the arrest. The Detectives waited with drawn weapons to welcome them, and the two gangsters gave no resistance. Later, while being taken from the house, Hershon made a weak effort to escape. He received a lacerated scalp for his effort.

Hershon made the first confession. He told the officers in detail about the shooting and stated that the third man, Charles M. Curtis, did the shooting. He confessed to the officers that he first met Curtis the night before the hold-up. He had never seen the man before.

Patrolman Dingman was twenty-eight years old at the time of his death. He had been with the Police Department for six years. He left a widow and a five-year-old son. He had been a life-long resident of Kansas City, Missouri.

The three gangsters were taken before Judge A. Stanford Lyon and arraigned for the murder of Officer Dingman. Judge Lyon forestalled any move the three gangsters might have made to plead guilty and slip through with a sentence to life imprisonment. "I want you to know," Judge Lyon said as the gangsters Watson, Hershon, and Curtis were arraigned before him, "that if you plead guilty I will sentence you to hang." Their trials were set for December 16, 1929. After hearing the judge, the three gangsters lost considerable blandness. Watson was inclined to be philosophical about it and talked to newsmen. It was he who fired the shots that killed Dingman. Hershon was also shooting, but Watson insisted he was a much better marksman than Hershon and was certain his bullets found a mark. Hershon was perfectly willing to allow Watson to make the claim. "It's a tough break," Watson said. "I was almost sure I had bumped off a 'copper,' and when I went home that night I told a friend I had. Well, it's just the result of trying to get by without working. We'd have been a lot better off if we had gone to work after we got out of stir."

Watson, Hershon, and Curtis were interviewed by the

Figure 75
Unidentified motorcycle patronmen (both photos)
Hugh Chase Private Library

prosecutors and asked, "What do you want to do?"

"Anything to save my neck," Watson replied.

The same question was asked of the others. Hershon affirmed Watson's proposal. However, Curtis said he desired to talk to his wife first. However, a moment later, he fell in with his companions and offered to plead guilty to first-degree murder.

"So," the prosecutor said, "you want to plead guilty, take life imprisonment, and save your necks because you are guilty?"

"Yes," in concert.

"Well," the prosecutor said, "let me tell you something. You're not going to get the chance. You are going to trial on first degree murder charges, with the death penalty staring you in the face; and we are going to do our best to see that you get it."

If possible, the three gangsters slumped a little farther into their chairs, but that was all.

In the same building where the men were sitting, four other men convicted of killing police officers were behind bars … awaiting their executions.[1]

---

1 *Kansas City Times,* December 4, 1929

MOUNTED PATROL

IT WAS APRIL 1929, when Kansas City's Police Department discussed replacing the mounted patrol in favor of more modern and efficient methods of patrolling the downtown area. A reporter for one of the local papers interviewed Mr. James McManamin at that time. James McManamin was the first police officer to mount a horse under a helmet adorned with the insignia of the City of Kansas City Missouri. At the time he started, the metropolis boasted a population of 125,000. Astride a huge bay named Richard, he moved down Grand Avenue at a "running walk" on official business.

Mr. McManamin worked when he was a boy as a mule car driver from the wharf to the landing, fares being 5, 10, and 15 cents. There were turntables at each end of the line. One day in May 1880, as young McManamin was at Fourth and Main turning the car around near Police Headquarters, Chief of Police Thomas Speers, the personification of law and order, hailed the mule car driver. "Your name McManamin?" The young lad gave an affirmative nod. "Well, I've got a job for you right now," stated Chief Speers. The young Irishman gave another nod. He accepted a police job at that moment. He drove his mule back to the barns at Twentieth Street and Grand Avenue and gave a spur of the moment resignation, leaving his superintendent to finish out his day. McManamin began his assigned duties at once. He served legal papers and patrolled the entire city.

Figure 76 — Mounted Patrol on parade
Photo: Hugh Chase Private Library

The young officer took many long rides on Richard. When the James boys, (Jessie and Frank) and their gang held up a Chicago and Alton train just west of Blue Springs in 1881, McManamin and his huge bay joined the posse that searched in vain for the train robbers. In 1885, Richard was sold and McManamin quit.

The mounted patrol grew to forty-five in number and made their last appearance as a body on Labor Day, 1929. The mounted policemen became a familiar sight, bringing a feeling of security to the hearts of citizens. They appeared in every parade held on the city streets for many years. They acted as escort to Queen Marie of Rumania, President Coolidge, Colonel Charles Lindburg, and many other dignitaries. The Kansas City mounted patrol took second place in show and competition at the Louisiana Purchase Exposition held in St. Louis, Missouri in 1904.

In 1927, August Vollmer, then Chief of Police of Berkley, California, conducted a survey of the police department at the request of the Board of Police Commissioners. He recommended that the mounted patrol be discontinued. In September 1929, good old "Pete" and "Spark Plug" along with the rest of the twenty-six mounts no longer reported for duty. Daisy, LuAnne, Jerry and Poncho turned in their equipment. Prince, Roger, Major and all the other "Blue Coats'" mounts equaled a handful of checks totaling $2,890.00.

Pete, Queen and Nellie had been fine officers. They pranced with pride in the parades. They twitched their ears at obtuse angles when their masters handed those little yellow tickets to people who double-parked, or to shoppers who forgot the time and parked too long. The auction block demanded its grist, without giving thought to the bond of love and emotion between mount and officer. Police Commissioners wagged their heads over mounting costs of operating the Police Department. They found that mounts "Rock" and "Judge," along with "Boy," ate too much. Alas, Chubby and Ben! Yes, Ben liked his oats and a nibble of lettuce from

Figure 77 — Unknown Mounted Officer
Photo: Hugh Chase Private Library

Figure 78 — Officers of Mounted Patrol
Photo: Hugh Chase Private Library

children at the city market when his Master rode out from Headquarters for their tour of duty downtown. Yes indeed, the Police Commissioners put their tongue in their cheeks when they found that Prince and Chick, as well as the other officers of the saddle and bridle, ate $40.00 worth of food each month. So, Colonel P.M. Gross took the gavel in his heavy fist. What was he doing? Who were these men gaping and prodding Spark Plug's flanks? See here, you can't do that to an officer!

Bang, bang, bang went the gavel. "What am I offered for this fine horse?" Colonel Gross was stuttering, the words falling fast. "Hey, hey, I've got $50.00. Who will make it $60.00?" When the task was done, Pet and Spark Plug and old gentle Ben were led away. The checks were counted—$2,890.00 for the horses. Yes, they are just horses now. Why certainly, Rock, you and old Chief have turned in your equipment. And Gyp and LuAnne, wonder where they are? Someone said they are at the auction place at 233 West Third Street. But men, we are officers; our place is downtown with the crowds, with the rattle and bank of life. Wise old Major knows all about it. He nuzzles his long time pal, Jerry. What are they shouting? Sturdy Mabel goes to the man who pays

Figure 79
Collage of Mounted Patrol
Photo: Hugh Chase Private Library

$250.00. She brought the top price of the sale. Mabel will continue to live in the city. LuAnne brought $200.00. Pete would move to the country and her new owner laid out $190.00. Roy and Jerry along with Major brought prices ranging from $60.00 to $70.00. A red line under the figure $40.00. The auction block, the gaping men, and the laughing onlookers: How could this be with fine officers leaving the service?

CHIEF LOUIS SIEGFRIED

LOUIS M. SIEGFRIED was appointed to the office of Chief of Police April 24, 1930. He served Kansas City in that position until April 1, 1932. Siegfried started with the department as a patrolman and worked himself up through the chain of command to the rank of assistant chief of police under Chief John L. Miles. Governor Caufield had just appointed Russell Fields and August F. Behrendt to the Board of Police Commissioners. He gave them instructions to select as chief of police a man capable of conducting an immediate and relentless campaign against major crimes occurring in Kansas City at that time. The Board felt Louis Siegfried was the man best qualified to carry out such an assignment.

The newly appointed chief soon found that enforcement of the law and prevention of crimes was just a small part of the problems that accompanied the responsibility of his office. Nineteen hundred thirty was a very hard year of the great depression. Money was scarce for everyone. Siegfried, a Republican Chief, tried to carry out the duties of his office with a Democratic machine as head of, and running, the city. This proved to be a giant hurdle and a pain of contention throughout his tenure as Chief of Police.

Twelve days after he took his oath of office, Judge McElroy (city manager) told him that the coffers of the general fund did not hold enough money to pay his officers. Theatrical company representatives offered to give a benefit performance to raise the $106,000.00 due the officers in back pay. Chief Siegfried declined the offer. He believed his officers had earned the wages and were not charity cases. He felt the city could (and should) find another means of raising payment. The Missouri Supreme Court handed down a decision that the city must furnish all monies necessary to operate an efficient police system.

Chief Siegfried's talents, abilities, administrative and diplomatic skills were constantly tested. Traffic fatalities broke previous records in 1931. A violent wave of crime seemed to close in on Kansas City. Part of the blame could be placed on the depression that caused mass unemployment.

Shortly after his appointment as Chief, a group of young hoodlums strutted along a strip of Independence Avenue between Highland and Grand Avenue. They openly carried weapons, threatened merchants, and beat any citizen who dared walk that district alone. One young man drove through that area, taking his family for a drive. Some young hoodlums, just for laughs, threw water on them as their vehicle slowed at an intersection. The young man stopped his automobile and protested. They repeated the water treatment, so he appealed to the police for protection. The police arrested three of his annoyers. They made bond and were on the street again within a short time. The young man who issued the complaint was murdered in his home before an hour had lapsed. About the same time, in the same general area, four men with baseball bats attacked two salesmen for the Helzberg Diamond Shop. Since five thousand dollars in diamonds remained untouched, this act could only be interpreted as sadism and cruelty. Chief Siegfried assigned six of his largest and most muscular men to patrol in that district. Armed with batons and orders to bring peace back to the area, that stretch of real estate soon became peaceful, quiet, and safe on Independence Avenue.

On June 18, 1931, the first radio communication was ini-

Figure 80 — Chief Louis M. Siegfried
Photo: Hugh Chase Private Library

tiated for police in Kansas City. Chief Siegfried was the first voice of record to speak officially to patrol officers deployed in district police cars. Harold Anderson, police dispatcher and Chief of Police ten years later, spoke second. This radio communication was a big step in the revolution of police methods.

In July 1931, City Manager McElroy stopped the practice begun in 1925 of remitting fifty cents from each traffic ticket or fine assessed to the Police Relief Association. This resulted in a loss of $25,000.00 to the Relief Association. This left the Association, which aided widows and officers in time of death or illness, with no method of funding. Members of the department regarded this as retaliation to the Mandamus Suit to compel the city to appropriate the amount necessary to operate the police department.

In 1931, prohibition was the law. Chief Siegfried and his officers received calls daily to enforce the law against bootlegging. More often than not raids on these dealers in illegal liquor involved gun battles. Some ended in casualties or death. Speak-easys and gambling establishments sprang up in the city like a plague. Siegfried and his officers attempted to stay on top of these establishments and forced them closed shortly after they opened. He received suggestions that he turn his head to some of these illegal establishments. In response, he concentrated harder. He closed any who went in business outside the law.

On March 15, 1932, the Supreme Court of Missouri ruled to return the police department to the provision of the city charter on the grounds that the law under which the department was operating under state supervision was unconstitutional. When the department returned to home rule, statistics showed that under Chief Siegfried and state control the police department compiled an excellent record. Burglaries and robberies plummeted more than one hundred percent compared to previous years. The crime picture took such a reduction that the risk companies reduced their rates to the Kansas City businessmen by fifty percent.

Chief Siegfried's troubles seemed to multiply with each day of the transition from state control to home rule. The first day the officers were to be paid after the city took control, the men were ordered to the city auditor's office to complete a personal (and supposedly confidential) individual questionnaire before they could draw their pay. These questionnaires later became reasons for dismissal of many of the officers. The remaining officers were very disgruntled and very unsure of their job security.

By October 1931, Kansas City was at the mercy of many bombings. Several theaters were having stiff labor disputes with unions when the unions were unable to organize and they continued hiring non-union employees. The people responsible for the bombings were not caught, and Chief Siegfried and the police department came under pressure and harsh criticism.

On October 7, 1931, the police arrested two burglars who were well equipped to cope with the modern police radio system and turn it into a definite advantage. They had two receivers tuned to the police wavelength. When one of the gang reached the intended crime scene, he placed a call back to the apartment they used as headquarters. In the apartment, a radio was tuned to pick up police broadcasts. It sat in front of the telephone transmitter. Using this complex method to their advantage, the criminals determined if they were in any danger.

Chief Siegfried found after the city and Judge McElroy began dictating policy to the police department that any raids made on gamblers or bootleggers would be released in the courts. Siegfried felt, but was unable to prove, this action was taken to ridicule him. In spite of the obstacles, the police department received praise for their work and the marked improvement shown in efficiency in the report by Walter Matscheack, of the Civic Research Institute, Berkeley, California. This report stated that although the police department had been the object of ridicule, a football for politics, and a joke for criminals, obviously far from perfect, but had climbed from one of the poorer ranking departments to one that was favorable to the best in the country.

Chief Siegfried resigned April 1, 1932. He served the community with honor through some very trying and troublesome times. History shows he was a giant of a man who rose on many occasions to show he was more than capable of a big job.

BILL ROBEEN

IT WAS MONDAY, August 24, 1931. George Rayen and Bill Robeen were assigned as investigators out of the office of Chief of Police Lewis M. Siegfried. These two young detectives went to check an alleged beer flat reported open for business at 1311 East Thirteenth Street. This was during the time of prohibition and both these eager detectives were ready to do anything they considered proper and legal to carry out their assigned duties. The two investigators were aware of the fact that this particular beer flat was raided frequently and that the residents and operators of the illegal establishment had become very cautious. Before a stranger gained entrance, he needed to be a personal acquaintance of the owners and operators of the flat.

Armed with this information, the two young officers soon found themselves ringing the doorbell at 1311 East Thirteenth Street. As they stood waiting for someone inside to answer the door, thoughts raced through their heads as to what approach might work to con their way inside. Presently from a small peephole drilled in the door, two very unfriendly eyes peered out at them. "You can't come in here," a gruff voice told the officers. "This isn't a visiting day."

The two officers made a weak attempt to argue with the owner of the piercing eyes. They found it impossible to argue successfully through a heavy oak door. They soon discovered their effort was gaining them nothing, so they walked away. They turned the corner and walked slowly down the street in silence. They were concentrating on their failure when they noticed a young man strolling and strumming a ukulele, giving his personal rendition of "Whistling in the Dark." He was so engrossed in his music that he never noticed the officer as he approached. Robeen's mind clicked like a beetle, and an idea struck. He summoned the musician. "We would like to serenade some friends," he told the young musician. "We will pay you fifteen cents cash to play the 'uke' while we sing."

The musician expressed a deep desire for the fifteen cents. He had trouble deciding what the policemen could sing. The young fellow with the ukulele knew only two songs. This limited the program Bill Robeen had in mind. The lad said he could play "Whistling in the Dark."

"But we don't know the words to that," Robeen objected.

"How about 'Sweet Adeline'?" "Sweet Adeline," the old stand-by of the village barbershop and moonlight nights, "was out." The man with the ukulele had never mastered "Sweet Adeline" on his instrument. "But I can play 'Springtime in the Rockies,' " he said, "if you gentlemen can sing it." The two officers informed the musician they knew all the words to "Springtime in the Rockies."

The musician with the ukulele and the two investigators made their way back to 1311 East Thirteenth Street. Once on the scene, they lined up and stood ready in front of the door. The musician bore down resolutely on the ukulele with all the talent he possessed. The two investigators, in tones reminiscent of a pinched buzz saw and an agitated jackass, gave voice to the words.

They just started their entertainment when a window of the flat flew up and a head protruded. "For the love of Pete," said a man later identified as Hogan, "who got hurt? What's all the noise about?"

"Yes," said a feminine voice, "what are you trying to do?"

"We're entertainers," said Robeen, the police department optimist.

"We're singing," said Rayen stoutly.

"Well," resumed the man with his head sticking from the window, "I'm glad you informed us. If that's what you're doing out there, come in before the police think it's a disturbance and start an investigation." The door opened. Robeen and Rayen, the musician and his treasured ukulele went inside. Once inside Robeen and Rayen displayed their badges. The musician unobtrusively slipped out the door with his ukulele and his fifteen cents. He exited so abruptly that his name was never known. They arrested the woman identified as Mrs. Shea and the man who gave his name as Hogan for operating a beer flat.

POLICE RADIO

THE KANSAS CITY Police Department first used radio communication to get calls to patrolmen assigned duty in district cars on June 18, 1931. This gave a tremendous time advantage previously unheard of. This meant that information and instructive orders went to officers in the field immediately. As any experienced officer can understand, time usually means the difference in solving a crime as well as conducting an arrest and apprehension of perpetrators.

A modern and complete radio system representing the most recent development in scientific communication became an adjunct to the Kansas City Police Department at noon, June 18, 1931. Its new transmitter station, KGPE, went on the air for continuous service. At noon that day, and for the few minutes that followed, the words of Chief Lewis M. Siegfried were heard in ten police stations, in thirty police vehicles on city streets, as well as by a few other key persons equipped with receivers to pick up the broadcasts. Only Chief Siegfried, Lieutenant Jack Hawley, the police drillmaster, and one of the three dispatchers of the new radio station—Patrolman Jack Ruddell, were allowed in the small studio at police headquarters as the Chief delivered his brief inaugural address.

As the clock struck twelve, Chief Siegfried spoke. He chose his words carefully and his strong voice carried over the airwaves. "This is Lewis M. Siegfried, Chief of the Metropolitan Police Department of Kansas City. I am speaking to all

Figure 81 — Kansas City, Missouri Police Department Parade

members of the Police Department and others of the radio audience. It gives me great pleasure to have the duty of announcing the official opening at this time of the Metropolitan Police Department's radio station. Through the experience of the police departments of other cities, this event heralds a marked improvement in the efficiency of this department. The installation of this equipment and the use of this system, however, will not prove successful in our work without the co-operation of the entire department. Each officer who has a duty to perform in the functioning of the system will be held strictly responsible for that particular task and should bear in mind that, without his individual effort toward complete harmony and co-operation, this system will be incomplete and unsuccessful."

Following Chief Siegfried's statement, the first message went out over the air from the lips of Lieutenant Hawley, whose voice carried clear and crisp, "Stand by for the first announcement." These words were repeated three times, "Officer J.A. Burkhardt, call your captain. This is station KGPE broadcasting." Forty-five seconds after the last word, Patrolman Burkhardt called Captain M.G. Succrow at police headquarters. In affixing numbers to various motor cars of the city, the car Burkhardt occupied was overlooked. Captain Succrow informed him that the identification number of his car was ten.

When the station first went on the air, H.A. Larson, the station's chief engineer, operated the transmitter. The other two engineers were Barney Carlisle and Bernard Holbert. Besides Ruddell, the dispatchers were Harold Anderson, who later became the department's Chief of Police, and H.B. Braden. Kansas City, from that day on, added efficiency to twenty-four hour police service, with all calls received night and day broadcast directly to all cars within districts. Following Chief Siegfried's inaugural talk, he again requested all who desired to call the police department for emergency services were to call headquarters direct so the call went on the air through KGPE.

The station broadcast the correct time every fifteen minutes throughout each twenty-four hour period. This not only kept the officers aware of the correct time, but also permitted the officers a constant check of the radio equipment in

Figure 82 — Early Police Departent radio equipment
Photo: Hugh Chase Private Library

their respective cars. At the same time superiors checked on the district patrolmen. If the men in the cars did not hear the time signals, they would at once conclude something was wrong. If a car happened to be called later, and the officers failed to respond as directed, it was apparent the officers had not been listening. A supervisor then took corrective action on the matter.

Following the first announcement by Lieutenant Hawley, no calls came in the first hour of the station's official operation. The first crime bulletin went out from the station at 1:30 p.m. It concerned the theft of a motor car from Seventh Street and Grand Avenue. Although the car, a 1929 Ford, bore Texas license No. A-8-1617, it belonged to E.L. Lassiter, 58 Coal Mine Road, Leeds, Missouri. The police dispatcher gave the engine number as A814666. The crime bulletin went on the air within moments of the incoming report.

TURKEY

IN MID-NOVEMBER 1931, officers J.J. Kinzy and D.B. Hudson, working out of Westport Station, were assigned to patrol the vicinity of Thirty-Eighth Street and Wyandotte Avenue. Both officers weighed 225 plus pounds and were in demand to hold back a crowd or block a doorway. When they responded to a call at 3826 Wyandotte, they found their bulk a disadvantage for the task awaiting them.

Response to this call for assistance found the problem centered on a huge "Tom Turkey" held captive in the basement of Mrs. John Bovard, of that address. Mr. Turkey had an appointment that he was reluctant to keep with the Bovard family as the meat course of their Thanksgiving dinner. It was evident he had no desire to assume his place of honor.

Tom was a spirited young turkey, fresh from the farm near DeSoto, Kansas. His spirit was far from broken (and his wings unclipped) by his move to the city. As wistfully as the prisoner of Oscar Wilde's poem, Tom cast his eyes toward the little patch of blue framed by the basement window. Mr. Bovard's brother James noted that he was not on good terms with the turkey. Mr. Bovard related to police later that the turkey had interfered with him on several occasions when he went to the basement to tend the furnace.

For this reason, Mr. Bovard was apprehensive when the deliveryman arrived to put coal in the basement window, which doubled as a coal chute. He rushed to the basement to hold the turkey and prevent his escape. As soon as Tom sighted the open window, he began to struggle as if he had the strength of seven ostriches, overpowering Mr. Bovard and making good his escape through the open window. Mr. Bovard rushed from the house crying, "Stop him! That's our Thanksgiving dinner!"

Almost immediately, a posse of small boys formed around Mr. Bovard. They spied the big Tom Turkey in a tree nearby. Removing a clothesline rope belonging to a neighbor, Mr. Bovard formed it into a lariat and bravely advanced toward Tom. At the second the posse circled the tree, Mr. Tom Turkey took to the air. Mr. Tom then exhibited a few sideslips and a couple of barrel rolls for the benefit of the crowd, and then he set a straight course for Baltimore Avenue. Swinging the lariat of wire, Mr. Bovard gave chase with the posse of boys tagging close behind.

Meanwhile, cooler heads prevailed. Mr. Bovard stopped by a telephone and summoned the assistance of the Police Department. Shortly, police car number 60 sped down Baltimore Avenue, the radio babbling a medley about bank rewards, bandits and convicts. Out of the side of the windows of the police cruiser leaned Officers Kinzy and Hudson with fierce and determined countenances. Another car soon arrived on the scene bearing a photographer with tripod and camera. A reporter jumped out, clutching pencil and pad. Housewives on Baltimore Avenue rushed to their front porches armed with brooms. Children pressed their noses flat against their front windows. Here was drama! Here was life!

The turkey perched in the top of a tall tree. He gobbled defiance at law, order and any other barrier between him and his freedom. Officer Kinzy drew his pistol from beneath his coat. "There's only one thing to do," he said firmly. "We've got to let him have it!"

"Shoot him in the head! Shoot him in the head!" shouted Mr. Bovard. "He's our Thanksgiving dinner! Don't spoil him, he's private property."

Officer Kinzy lowered his weapon. "To shoot him in the head," he said, "I would need a rifle."

"I have a rifle somewhere!" exclaimed Mrs. C.R. Simpson of 3815 Baltimore Avenue, a curious and interested bystander.

"Where is the rifle?" inquired the policemen.

"I hid it someplace," said Mrs. Simpson. "I was afraid the children might get it."

"Wait here, everyone! Don't move!" commanded Officer Kinzy, vanishing in the house behind Mrs. Simpson. They searched first the attic, then the basement and the stairs, where she kept the mops and brooms. Finally, they found the rifle — a 22 caliber.

A surge swept through the spectators as officer Kinzy stepped out on the porch, armed and resolute. No one moved. Officer Kinzy raised the rifle. "Steady everyone! Steady!" said Officer Hudson. "Shoot him in the head!" exclaimed Mr. Bovard in a stage whisper. Slowly the blue barrel raised into position. Swiftly Mr. Tom Turkey took to the air circling and gobbling. He flew from view with an insolent flip of his tail feathers.

"Damn! I was just drawing a bead on him," exclaimed Officer Kinzy ruefully.

"After him, men," roared Officer Hudson.

The officers, the photographer, and the press piled into district car number 60. The car whisked east on Thirty-Eighth Street and south on Main Street. The busy traffic at Thirty-Ninth and Main opened like a suspension bridge. Mr. Bovard, with his wire lariat, took a shorter route across back yards and over back fences. An alert canine nearly bit him.

Mr. Tom Turkey completely disappeared from sight, but the chase continued. At Thirty-Seventh and Walnut Streets, the pursuers halted to take council.

"My theory," Officer Hudson said, "is that he is headed for a location with a lot of trees." "If I were a turkey," reasoned Kinzy, "I'd get as far away as possible. Let's go there."

The two officers dashed off toward Rockhill district, which has a dense growth of trees. Mr. Bovard scouted independently.

The scene of this drama then shifts to the Netherlands Hotel at 3835 Main Street. Jimmie Romondo, the bellboy, unaware of impending fame, was seated in the lobby. He happened to glance out and see a crowd gathered, craning their necks upward.

Jimmie Romondo walked outside to investigate. He glanced upward and instantly returned. "Give me the key to room #516," he told the girl at the switchboard.

"There are no guests in 516," she replied.

"That's what you think. There's a turkey in it."

"Heavens! One of our best rooms, too!" exclaimed the young lady.

Being a country turkey, this was his first time to check into a hotel. He was occupied with pecking at the bedspread when the uniformed bellboy entered the room and hurled himself on the visitor. Mr. Bovard arrived at that time and slipped the wire loop over Tom's head. Tom Turkey returned to the Bovard basement via police vehicle number 60 amidst excited cheers from the spectators. Mr. Turkey awaited Thanksgiving Day and his appointment with destiny in the basement.

UNION STATION MASSACRE

KANSAS CITY Police Detectives W.J. "Red" Grooms and his partner Frank Hermanson normally were assigned to the downtown area working burglaries. Both were veterans of the police department and were well respected as diligent, hard-working officers who had made numerous arrests and solved countless cases. They would dog a suspect until he was brought to justice. The criminal world of the 1930's feared these two men, who regularly used the police department's only armored car.

On the evening of June 16, 1933, their captain informed Detectives Grooms and Hermanson that the following morning they would be on special assignment. Both officers were to meet at Union Station with two special agents of the Justice Department and a police chief from Oklahoma. The officers were to assist in escorting a prisoner to Leavenworth, Kansas. A simple assignment — nothing to lose sleep over. In fact, this minor assignment would not require the usual police hardware that they normally checked out of the gunroom, such as a machine gun or shotgun.

Detectives Grooms and Hermanson arrived at the station at 6:55 a.m. on Saturday, June 17, 1933. They spotted the FBI Agents' vehicle, a 1933 Chevrolet Coach bearing Nebraska license plates, parked on the wide station drive. It was headed south into the curb opposite the Station's main south entrance. Detective Grooms pulled into the plaza parking area, turned into the curb directly in front of the Agents' vehicle, and parked. Approximately ten feet separated their front bumpers. By prearrangement, they walked into the lobby to meet with Special Agent Reed Vetterli and his partner Special Agent Raymond Caffrey. Upon meeting and exchanging greetings, the officers checked with the ticket agent to verify the arrival time of the Missouri Pacific train from Little Rock, Arkansas. They were told that it was on time and would arrive on track twelve. Special Agent Vetterli then informed the detectives that they were waiting for FBI Agents Joseph Lackey, Frank Smith, and the Police Chief of McAlester, Oklahoma, Otto Reed. This group had in custody Frank Nash, an escaped prisoner and vicious killer.

It was a beautiful, sunny day. The station was filled with more than the usual amount of travelers. Fred Harvey's Restaurant was doing a booming business serving coffee and breakfast. People waited for trains, leisurely enjoying the moment.

It was now 7:15 a.m. The night train from Little Rock was right on schedule. As it came to a halt, Special Agent Joe Lackey was the first to step onto the train platform. After checking the area visually, he motioned the two detectives and Agents Vetterli and Caffrey onto the train where they met with Agent Smith and the infamous prisoner Frank Nash. They discussed their plans, anticipating no real problems at the Station. The officers, agents, and prisoner then left the train and walked directly up the stairs and down the long corridor to the lobby. Special Agents Vetterli and Caffrey led the way, followed by Frank Nash, who was now surrounded by Special Agents Smith, Lackey, and Chief Reed. Detectives Grooms and Hermanson brought up the rear. Vetterli and Caffrey carried shotguns. Nash's hands were handcuffed in front of him. The agents placed a handkerchief over the handcuffs to avoid alarming the public, walked with their prisoner out of the Station, and crossed over to the Agents' parked car. As they started to load into the vehicle, three men approached and the loud staccato report of a machine gun broke the serenity of the morning. People scattered in all directions to escape the gunfire. Some hit the pavement and some the floor of their vehicles for protection. Many bystanders just stared in amazement.

Prior to the gunfire, the prisoner and his escorts had approached the vehicle from the rear. Detectives Grooms and Hermanson, now in front of them by a few feet, had headed off to the passenger side. They stopped near the front of the Agents' vehicle to wait for the passengers to load. Meanwhile, the two detectives talked idly with each other with their backs to the west.

Special Agent Joe Lackey, followed by prisoner Nash, Chief Reed, and Special Agent Smith, walked to the driver's door while Special Agents Vetterli and Caffrey stopped on the right side by the rear fender. They leaned their shotguns against the vehicle. Special Agent Vetterli awaited the loading of the others before climbing into the right front seat. He was now facing toward the detectives and conversing with them.

Special Agent Joe Lackey, in the meantime, opened the driver's door and prisoner Nash started to climb in the rear seat. Special Agent Lackey stopped him and told Nash to sit up front. Nash complied and temporarily seated himself behind the steering wheel to await Lackey's order. Lackey then entered the vehicle, seating himself in the left rear. Otto Reed entered next, climbing over Lackey to the right rear. Special Agent Smith then entered, passing over Reed, and took the middle position between Lackey and Reed.

At the same time, Special Agent Caffrey walked around the rear of the car to the driver's side door. Nash was instructed to slide over to the center, putting Nash between Vetterli and Caffrey. Caffrey was to drive. Detectives Grooms and Hermanson were starting to walk to their police vehicle in order to follow the others to Leavenworth, Kansas, as an escort.

At that precise second, two unknown men approached

from the front of the Agents' vehicle. One had a machine gun; the other was armed with a revolver. Both were in close range, just a few feet from the officers. To the rear and left, behind a concrete barrier, was a third man armed with a machine gun. In less than ten seconds, five men including Frank Nash were murdered.

A caseworker for the Travelers Aid assigned to Union Station witnessed the shootings at close range. She saw the prisoner and the officers before the shootings occurred and gave the following statement. "I followed the group onto the platform watching them make their way across the street. I saw them direct Nash into the front seat of the car. Right at that time I saw a large man weighing at least 200 pounds step out from behind the lamppost beside the concrete bus landing. He was carrying a gun. One of those with a cylinder on top of it. He started shooting right at the two officers. They never uttered a word. They just began shooting. At the same time, two men stepped out from behind my Oakland car, which was parked a little west of the officers. My car was facing to the north. Both men were small. One had what appeared to be a shotgun, the other a machine gun. They started shooting at the officers. The officers fell to the ground on the east side of the car in which Nash had been placed. One of the men started shooting right past Nash. I believe this was the man who killed Nash. The officers were the first to fall. Nash was the last one killed." The witness also testified that it was one of the detectives on the east side of the Chevrolet who began shooting at the gunmen behind her car.

Special Agent Frank Smith's statement gave the following testimony about the events of the shooting. "Lackey and Reed had both climbed into the rear seat. Lackey on the left and Reed on the right. I had just started to climb in behind them. Suddenly I heard someone shout, ... Put 'em up!" I drew my revolver and froze in a crouched position. I turned my weapon and pointed toward the direction from which I had heard the shouts. I saw a man blazing away with a machine gun and I dived for the floor and played dead. It was the only thing I could do. If that man had been armed with a six-shooter, I could have matched him with mine, but I knew he had a machine gun so I slumped down between Reed and Lackey. I felt my friend Reed sag on me. I looked up and Nash had been hit. His head was thrown back and his toupee had fallen from his head to the floor."

Contrary to the above statements, crime investigators have indicated that as Smith was bent over squeezing past Special Agent Lackey and into the center of the back seat of the vehicle, Special Agent Caffrey prepared to enter the front from the opposite side. The killers made their move. A gangster thought to be Charles Arthur Floyd, AKA Pretty Boy Floyd, took a step to the right of the vehicle he had been waiting beside, pointed his machine gun in the direction of Caffrey, and yelled at him "Put 'em up! Up! Up!" Another gangster, thought to be Adam Richetti, a sidekick of Floyd, started forward between their vehicle and the one he had been standing behind, revolver raised. A third gangster, thought to be Verne Miller, carrying a submachine gun, stepped up on the running board of a parked vehicle for a better view. As the command from Floyd rang out, Detectives Grooms and Hermanson were facing almost directly at Floyd across the hood of the Special Agents' vehicle. Without hesitation, Detective "Red" Grooms drew his revolver and fired, getting off two shots but missing Floyd. At this time Miller shouted, "Let 'em have it!" Miller was positioned to Grooms' right rear. Nash yelled to Floyd, "For God's sake! Don't shoot me!" Miller and Floyd opened up with merciless gunfire, pouring lead missiles into the bodies of the law enforcement officers. A massacre was now in progress and from that point on would be known as "The Union Station Massacre."

Special Agent Caffrey, still outside the door of the Chevrolet, fell to the ground dead. Frank Nash's head snapped against the back of the seat as he was hit in the face and chest. Floyd continued firing, walking slowly towards the car, now spraying the men in the rear of the vehicle. The muzzle of the Tommy gun swept back and forth in small, jerky movements.

Detectives Grooms and Hermanson were shot almost point blank by Verne Miller from the other side of the car, literally cutting both officers in half. Special Agent Vetterli was not hit in the first barrage. However, Adam Richetti now moved forward, shooting at Special Agent Vetterli — striking him in the arm and knocking him to the pavement. As Vetterli hit the pavement, he rolled partially under a vehicle to the west of him to take cover. As this happened Miller advanced towards the Agents' vehicle, transferring his fire directly into the back of their vehicle. The crossfire at this point was accurate and deadly. Special Agent Smith dove forward to the floor, feigning death. Chief Reed, on his right, slumped in the seat. He was riddled by bullets, his head nearly severed from his body. Special Agent Joseph Lackey, critically wounded with two bullets in his spine and one in his pelvis, fell over Special Agent Smith onto the rear floor.

Suddenly the gunfire ceased. The killers, in unison, rushed to the FBI vehicle and looked inside. One of the gangsters stated, "They're all dead. Let's get out of here!" The three gunmen ran toward their vehicle.

Police Officer M.K. (Mike) Fanning, a foot beat officer assigned to the Union Station area, emerged from the Station at a dead run. He had his revolver in hand. A witness to the shooting yelled at the officer, "There he is, Mike", pointing in the direction of the now fleeing Floyd. Officer Fanning took a kneeling position by a portico post and fired three shots at Floyd with his revolver. Floyd slumped briefly, but continued to run.

Special Agent Vetterli struggled to his feet. Although wounded, he was able to grab a shotgun from the front fender of the car and fired several shots at the escaping gangster's vehicle as it sped westward out of the plaza parking area. Officer Fanning, not knowing who was shooting at whom, ran to Special Agent Vetterli and demanded at gunpoint to know who he was. The agent identified himself. Officer Fanning turned his attention to the victims and realized that two of his brother officers were down. Detectives Grooms and Hermanson were laying on their backs in pools of blood. Both officers were dead. Officer Fanning, along with Special Agent Vetterli, checked the other agents and prisoner. They found that Nash was dead and Special Agent Caffrey was dead or dying. In the back seat of the Agents' vehicle Special Agent Smith was now sitting in the middle holding an arm under the head of Chief Otto Reed and talking to Special Agent Lackey, stating to him, "Steady, steady. You'll make it all right." Special Agent Lackey was conscious and moaning.

Crowds began to gather. Police and ambulance sirens could be heard in the distance. The momentarily hushed atmosphere was quickly changing. Special Agent Lackey and Caffrey were both taken by ambulance to Research Hospital where Special Agent Caffrey was pronounced dead on arrival and Lackey was received in the emergency room.

This cold-blooded murder made headlines all over the United States. It forced the FBI into unprecedented action. FBI Director J. Edgar Hoover had the United States Attorney General Cummings order every law enforcement agency under their jurisdiction to join in the manhunt for the killers. An FBI agent, two Kansas City detectives, and an Oklahoma Police Chief had been slain in the performance of their duty. Mr. Hoover's orders were brief and direct. "Produce the fugitives or prove them dead." Within hours of the massacre, special agents of the FBI swarmed into Kansas City, and one of the most intensive manhunts in the nation's history began.

On the Monday prior to the massacre, June 12, 1933, Chief Special Agent Joseph Kirby Ellis of the Missouri, Kansas, and Texas Railroad was preparing for his first vacation in twenty years. His telephone rang. Special Agent Frank Smith of the FBI was calling Ellis from Oklahoma City, Oklahoma. For the past several weeks Agents Smith and Ellis, along with Chief Special Agent John Burness of the Rock Island Railroad worked together on a tip concerning the location of Frank Nash, escaped murderer and train robber. Special Agent Smith informed Ellis that Nash had been spotted with his wife in Hot Springs, Arkansas. Smith requested that Ellis go with him to identify Nash since no other law enforcement officer was as familiar with the gangster. Ellis responded that he was not able to go as he was going on vacation and did not want to disappoint his wife. However, he informed Smith that Otto Reed, Chief of Police at McAlester, Oklahoma, knew Nash as well as he did and would be able to identify Nash for Smith. Special Agent Smith contacted Reed by telephone to explain the situation. Chief Reed elected to drive from McAlester to Oklahoma City to assist the FBI. Upon Reed's arrival in Oklahoma City on June 15, 1933, he and Special Agents Smith and Lackey made plans to capture Nash. They all three knew that any attempt to arrest Nash might be met with armed resistance from other gang members. In order to keep him from talking, the gangsters might eliminate him altogether.

On June 16, the three officers arrived in Hot Springs, Arkansas. They spotted Nash standing in front of the White Front Pool Hall. He was drinking a bottle of beer and talking to two men. Reed recognized Nash at once and identified him to the other agents. The officers arrested Nash. He was unarmed and offered no resistance. The officers rushed Nash to their waiting vehicle and headed toward Joplin, Missouri. As the officers expected to be pursued, they decided that once in Joplin they would double back to Little Rock. They arrived in Little Rock in the early evening. While there, they drove to the Police Department where Agent Smith placed two telephone calls. He placed the first call to J. Edgar Hoover in Washington, D.C., advising Hoover of the capture of Nash. The second call went to Special Agent Vetterli, who was in charge of the Kansas City FBI Office. Special Agent Smith informed him of Nash's arrest and requested that Vetterli meet with him and the other apprehending officers at Union Station at 7:15 a.m. on June 17. They would be arriving on the Missouri Pacific from Little Rock, Arkansas. Special Agent Smith further requested an armed escort from the train to the Leavenworth Penitentiary.

Only seconds after the apprehension of Nash, the criminal underworld started action. Word was sent to Richard Galatas, a Hot Springs gambler, con man, and personal friend of Frank Nash. Galatas immediately notified Nash's wife Frances at a tourist court in Hot Springs of his arrest. He informed her that it was thought the officers were taking him to Joplin, Missouri.

Mrs. Nash, after learning of the arrest of Frank, called Louis (Doc) Staci in Melrose Park, Illinois. He was a nightclub owner and operator. He was also known in the underworld as an "arranger" — someone who arranged for the murder of people that the criminal world paid to have killed. Although Staci was not a killer himself, he was acquainted with most of the killers in the country. He was the person who assigned a killer to do a job and paid them.

Mrs. Nash then made a second call to Herbert Farmer in Joplin, Missouri, who was also a gambler and friend of Frank Nash. At this time, speculation was that the law officers and Nash were headed for Joplin. It is thought that Farmer agreed to furnish the weapons and gunmen to liberate Nash at Joplin.

Mrs. Nash and Galatas then rented a plane and flew to Joplin, Missouri, where Farmer met them. He told them that the car transporting Nash had not been observed in the Joplin area. He and other elements of the underworld had the highways under surveillance since being informed of Nash's arrest. Farmer then drove Galatas and Frances to his home to await further developments. By evening, they were almost certain that Nash and the officers had by-passed Joplin. Mrs. Nash then placed a second phone call to Staci in Melrose Park, Illinois.

Staci thought that since Nash made good his escape from the Leavenworth Penitentiary he would probably be returned to the same penitentiary. He also thought they would most likely bring Nash through Kansas City. Staci then telephoned Frank B. (Fritz) Malloy, a Kansas City bootlegger, and inquired about hiring Kansas City gunmen. Malloy told Staci if the price was right he could persuade John Lazia (mob boss of the Kansas City underworld and running the Police Department), to make some type of deal. He also told Staci to contact Verne Miller, a contract killer and close friend of Frank Nash. He was in Kansas City and might help Staci.

Within a short time, Malloy called Staci back with information from underworld sources that FBI Agent Smith's telephone conversation with Special Agent Vetterli had been overheard and passed on to Malloy. Staci was further informed that John Lazia refused to help. Lazia didn't want the heat that would come down on Kansas City's underworld as a result of freeing Nash. However, Lazia did tell Malloy how Nash would arrive, the precise time, who was with him, and that Nash would be taken directly to the Leavenworth Penitentiary. It is thought that Lazia learned this information from Chief of Detectives Otto P. Higgins, who was on Lazia's payroll. Chief Higgins, in turn, had earlier been telephoned by Special Agent Vetterli, advising him of the capture of Frank Nash by the FBI and requesting some officers to meet the Missouri Pacific train at 7:15 a.m. to assist with escorting Nash by vehicle to Leavenworth. The Chief agreed to loan two detectives for this assignment.

Verne Miller was contacted by Malloy and stated the situation. Miller suggested the best time to liberate Nash was while they were entering the car in the Union Station parking lot. However, he could not do it alone and needed help.

About the same time the FBI Agents were traveling to Hot Springs, Arkansas, two criminals arrived in Boliver, Missouri, in a stolen vehicle. They had earlier shot and killed a Missouri State Trooper and a Sheriffs Officer in Columbia, Missouri. One criminal was Charles Arthur (Pretty Boy) Floyd. The other was his partner Adam Richetti. Floyd was a killer and small time gangster who gained fame through the media's glorification of his deeds as a bank robber and gunman. He was considered nothing more than a "smalltime punk" by the elite underworld of the 1930's. Adam Richetti was a cruel killer who enjoyed killing.

The two gangsters drove to a garage where they were acquainted with the owner. Upon arrival, they found their friend having morning coffee with Polk County Sheriff Jack Killingsworth. When the gangsters realized that Killingsworth was a law enforcement officer, they pulled their guns on him. The two gangsters decided to kill the sheriff but the garage owner talked them out of it. He told Floyd he would consider it a personal favor if he let the sheriff live. Floyd then took another vehicle from the garage. He decided to take the sheriff with them as an afterthought. Floyd showed his disrespect of the small town sheriff by never disarming him.

At some point on the trip, Floyd stopped another vehicle at gunpoint and commandeered the vehicle and operator. Floyd now had two captives. They drove to Lee's Summit, Missouri, where the gangsters treated their two captives to dinner. After dinner, Floyd released the two captives with instructions to stay in the car and not report the incident for a few hours. They complied.

Floyd and Richetti stole a third vehicle while in Lee's Summit and drove on to Kansas City. Upon arrival in Kansas City, they contacted the Northside Political Headquarters and attempted to contact John Lazia. However, they got Lazia's lieutenant, a gangster by the name of "Gus" Gargotta. Floyd, as a courtesy to Lazia, was letting them know that he and Adam Richetti were in town. Floyd was requested to get in touch with Verne Miller. Floyd and Richetti spent the night of the sixteenth at Miller's residence, 6612 Edgevale Road. Evidence gathered later at that address showed the three men's fingerprints on beer bottles. It is assumed that they discussed how best to liberate Nash and made plans to do so. Miller telephoned Farmer in Joplin and Staci in Melrose Park stating they would free Frank Nash. However, it is not known whether they were planning to liberate Nash or kill him to insure his silence.

That question will never be answered. Miller, Floyd, and Richetti drove to Union Station on June 17, 1933, locating both the FBI vehicle and the Kansas City Detectives' vehicle. Either by chance or by arrangement, the three gangsters parked next to the Kansas City Detectives' vehicle. The stage was set to free Frank Nash.

The investigation of this incident at Union Station positively identified Miller, Richetti, and Floyd as the three gunmen. The FBI, through their intense and thorough investigation, implicated at least a dozen other suspects. The FBI secured eleven indictments: Miller, Richetti, and Floyd for homicide, Herbert Farmer and his wife Esther, Louis Staci, Frances Nash, Richard Galatas and wife Elizabeth, Fritz Malloy, and Vivian Mathias (Miller's girlfriend) for conspiracy to obstruct justice.

Verne Miller's nude body was recovered from a ditch near Detroit, Michigan, in November of 1933. His head was crushed and his legs drawn tight against his torso by repeated wrappings with clothesline. There were marks on his throat indicating he had been garroted.

Charles Floyd and Adam Richetti were caught near Wellsville, Ohio, on October 20, 1934. Floyd was driving a Ford Tudor. It was damp and foggy; the vehicle skidded into a telephone pole near Wellsville. They were traveling with two women, Beulah and Rose Baird. They sent the women into the city with the vehicle to have it repaired. The two gangsters hid out in a wooded area on Alonzo Israel's farm.

A farmer reported to Wellsville Police that he had spotted Floyd and Richetti. They investigated and a major gun battle ensued. Richetti was wounded and captured. Pretty Boy Floyd escaped. Floyd, on foot, started south staying away from town and the highway. He made his way to an isolated farm and asked for food and a ride to Youngstown. While he waited for a ride on the front porch of the farmhouse, the FBI and local law officers surrounded Floyd. He was told to surrender but instead took off running. He was then shot down. Floyd died shortly after being shot.

Adam Richetti was returned to Kansas City, Missouri, for trial. He was charged with the murder of Detective Frank E. Hermanson. On June 17, 1935, the jury returned a verdict of guilty. The court ordered Richetti to death. On October 7, 1938, Adam Richetti was put to death in the gas chamber at the Missouri State Penitentiary in Jefferson City, Missouri.

In 1936, these words appeared in the Kansas City Star. *"The long arm of the government is reaching a protective arm around the widows of the two Kansas City Detectives, William J. Grooms and Frank E. Hermanson, who were slain in the Union Station Massacre, June 17, 1933. Word has been received in Kansas City that the Claims Committee of the House of Representatives reported favorably today a bill to pay Mrs. Grooms and Mrs. Hermanson $5,000.00 each. Representative C. Jasper Bell, who introduced the measure in Washington, stated he was positive the two claims would be paid by Congress this winter."* The bill was defeated.

Figure 83 — Crime Scene Photo 1
Photo: Hugh Chase Private Library

Figure 84 — Crime Scene Photo 2
Photo: Hugh Chase Private Library

Figure 85 — Crime Scene Photo 3
Photo: Hugh Chase Private Library

Figure 86 — Crime Scene Photo 4
Photo: Hugh Chase Private Library

Figure 87 — Crime Scene Photo 5
Photo: Hugh Chase Private Library

Figure 88 — Crime Scene Photo 6
Photo: Hugh Chase Private Library

Figure 89 — Crime Scene Photo 7
Photo: Hugh Chase Private Library

Figure 90 — Crime Scene Photo 8
Photo: Hugh Chase Private Library

Figure 91 — Crime Scene Photo 9
Photo: Hugh Chase Private Library

Figure 92 — Crime Scene Photo 10
Photo: Hugh Chase Private Library

Figure 93 — Crime Scene Photo 11
Photo: Hugh Chase Private Library

Figure 94 — Crime Scene Photo 12
Photo: Hugh Chase Private Library

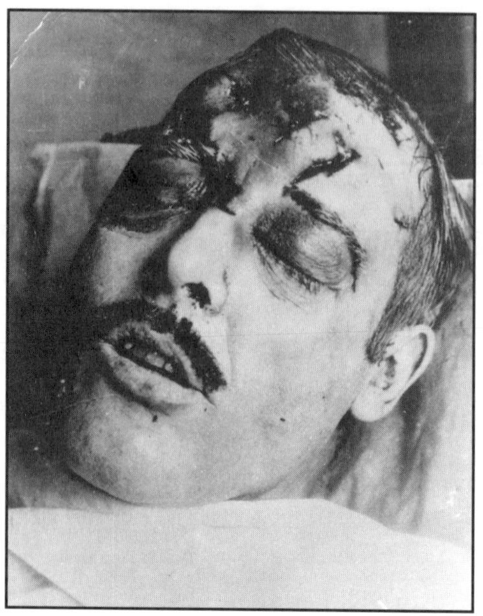

Figure 95 — Crime Scene Photo 13 (Frank Nash)
Photo: Hugh Chase Private Library

Figure 96 — Crime Scene Photo 14
Photo: Hugh Chase Private Library

Figure 97 — Federal Agents R.E. Vetterli (left) and Frank Smith (right)
Photo: Hugh Chase Private Library

ureau of Investigation
ent of Justice
ngton, D. C.
Certify
Caffrey
otograph appear hereon, is a regu-
pecial Agent
reau of Investigation, Department of Justice, and as such is
investigating violations of the laws of the United States and
in which the United States is or may be a party in interest.
Attorney General.

Figure 98 — FBI Special Agent Raymond Caffrey's official ID
Hugh Chase Private Library

Figure 99 — Special Agent Raymond J. Caffrey
Photo: FBI Hall of Honor

Figure 100 — Special Agent F. Joseph Lackey
Photo: FBI Archives

Figure 101 — McAlester, OK Police Chief Otto Reed
Photo: Kansas City Library Special Collection

Figure 102 — Kansas City Detective W.J. (Red) Grooms
Photo: Kansas City, Missouri Police Department

Figure 103 — Kansas City Detective Frank Hermanson
Photo: Kansas City, Missouri Police Department

Figure 104 — Rose (left) and Beulah (right) Baird
Photo: FBI Archives

Figure 105 — (Top row) Charles Arthur "Pretty Boy" Floyd, Adam Richetti and (bottom) Verne Miller
Photos: FBI Historic Famous Cases

Figure 106 — Frank Nash
Photo: www.crimelibrary.com/ gangsters2

Figure 107
Vivian Mathias
(Verne Miller's girlfriend)
Photo: Hugh Chase Private Library

Figure 108
Vivian Mathias
(Verne Miller's girlfriend)
and daughter Betty
http://www.fortunecity.com/meltingpot/kuwait/55id28_m.htm

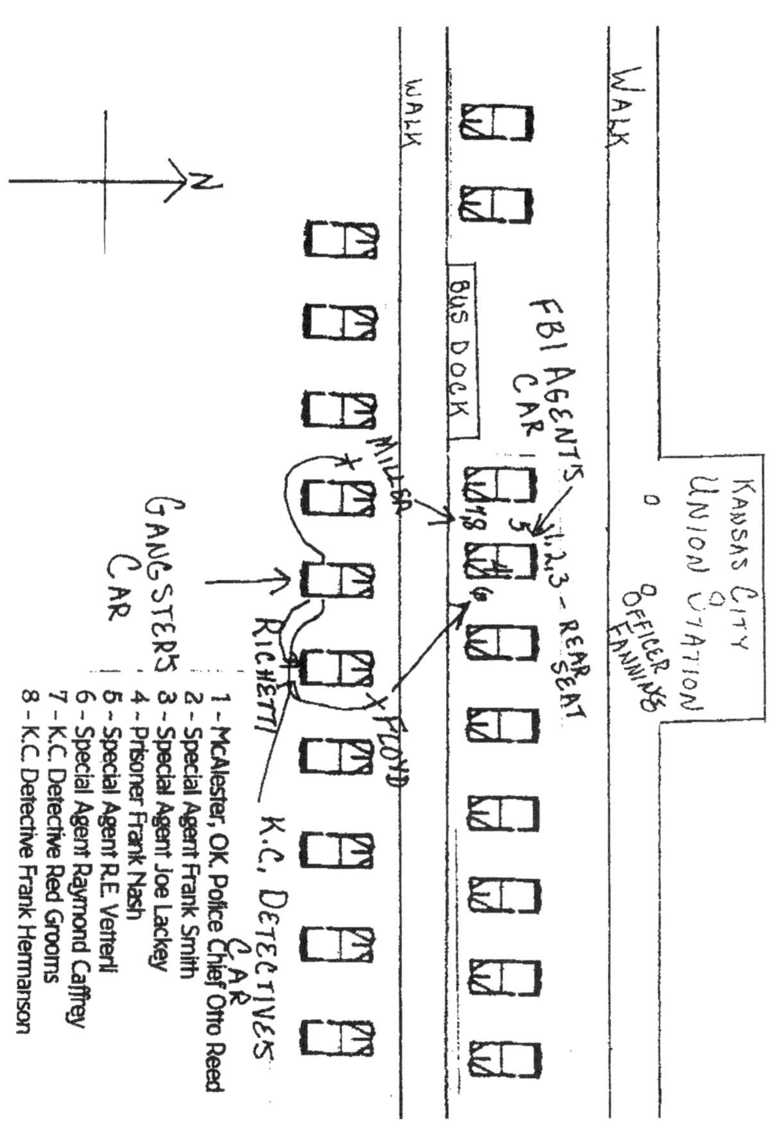

Figure 109 — Union Station Crime Scene Diagram —

TATTOO GANG

A DOZEN MEN, who found themselves at the bottom of the social ladder, remained unaware that they wore a brand of death. A crafty plotter wove their lives into an evil web and waited at the center like a spider to feast on his fellow man's flesh.

When they first saw the cabalistic tattoo, it impressed Detectives John P. Clifford, Jr. and John F. Flavin only through routine curiosity. It later became a challenge, a lock which no key seemed to fit. These two young detectives were working in the old headquarters at Fourth and Main Streets on a summer afternoon in 1935. An anonymous caller reported that a bandit was hidden in a flophouse nearby. This call took them to a squalid district of town made up of greasy slum joints, nickel grog shops, rescue missions, and odor-reeking hotels where canvas cots cost a dime a night and a cubbyhole two times that price.

Within minutes after receiving the call, the two officers busted into one of these places with drawn guns. A specter reeking of "derail" (rotgut alcohol and water which sold on the north side for 15 cents a pint), roused from an iron bed and stared at them in a stupor. Clifford spat in disgust, "This bottle hound couldn't hold up his little finger."

The bum on the bed wheezed, "You'll not refuse an old, sick man the price of coffee and...," his voice trailed off and tears glistened in the bloodshot eyes. "It's been three days since I..." The detectives knew this man well as "Crying Hank."

After a short conversation, Flavin asked about a strange mark Hank bore on his arm. Flavin took out a small pocket penlight to get a closer look at the tattoo it displayed.

"Harry H. Burke," Flavin read aloud. There was a birth date beneath the name and still another line, "Twenty eight Nineteen East Ninth, K.C. Remember?" Flavin prodded.

"Sure," replied Clifford. "We made a call on Fifth Street on that D.O.A. It was the same except for the name and date." The two detectives, feeling something amiss, questioned Hank about the tattoo. Hank told them that a man by the name of "Charley Kelly" had him put it on his arm. Clifford and Flavin returned to headquarters perplexed. They wondered why tattoos suddenly became a fad among the rum-dums. These alcoholics usually thought only about their next drink. The tattoos stuck in the detectives' minds and could not be dismissed.

On March 8, Clifford and Flavin were dispatched to another cheap hotel where a dead body had been found. This type of call to a fleabag hotel was not unusual. Dope, rotten liquor, malnutrition, exposure to weather, sleeping on the sidewalks and in doorways causes a high mortality rate among these people.

The investigation by Detectives Clifford and Flavin re-

Figure 110 — 1933 Department Fleet at foot of Qulity Hill
Photo: Hugh Chase Private Library

Det. Clifford

Det. Flavin

Figure 111 — *The Informant October 1971*

vealed a man with glassy eyes staring sightlessly at the ceiling. Like many of the others in that district, the detectives knew him. He was George "Cyclone" Kelly. Years before he had been a boxer of some reputation. He, like many of the derelicts, once enjoyed both success and money. Then he drank everything away and became a bum and a panhandler. Cause of death was apparent, so no autopsy was performed. The alert detectives noticed one unusual thing about the body. On the dead man's right arm was a curious tattoo: his birth date and an address of 2819 East Ninth Street.

Thinking it might be the address of relatives, Clifford and Flavin went to the two-story residence at 2819 East Ninth Street. When they rang the doorbell, they waited a few minutes. Soon a gentleman responded who identified himself as Charles D. Ernest. When they explained their mission, Mr. Ernest informed them they must have made a mistake. He had never even heard of George (Cyclone) Kelly.

Clifford and Flavin were in their office reviewing details

of the prizefighter's death. After seeing the second tattoo on Burke, they stumbled onto another coincidence. They made a telephone call to another officer, a friend who left the department to become an insurance investigator. A few days before they met their friend emerging from the Carr House at 514 Main, another cheap hotel truthfully described as a flophouse. At that meeting, he told the detectives he was looking for someone but failed to say whom.

"It is George, alias Charles Kelly, I am looking for," the investigator informed them over the phone. "So far no luck. I haven't found any trace of him."

"Come on down," said Flavin, "maybe we can give you a tip or supply a lead."

Closeted with the detectives, the insurance representative listened to the report about the tattoo on crying Hank's arm, and that Charley Kelly told him to have it done! The investigator inquired, "Did you find out where Kelly lives?"

The officers called on Burke again, but the man was unable to give them any helpful information. Charles Kelly was a swell guy and always willing to pass along the price of a pint. "He is a swell fellow," insisted crying Hank, who had earned his nickname for his ability to turn on the tears when he saw an opportunity to mooch a dime.

Kelly, the insurance sleuth told the detectives, was a brother of Cyclone Kelly, the boxer. "My company carried a life insurance policy on the boxer," he explained. "That's why I am trying to locate his brother."

Hardly a week passed after Clifford and Flavin burst in on "Crying Hank" in search of a bandit when another anonymous telephone call sent them to another flophouse on the trail of the phantom stickup man. They felt the tip was phony, but they could not ignore it. Their raid netted yet another "derail" soaked bum who bore the tattoo. Other false calls followed, but they always found bearers of the tattoos.

The detective team started a search for the artist who had inscribed the tattoos. They soon learned that James

Malcolm, who operated a small establishment in a north side hotel, had made the tattoos. When asked if he had been doing work for Charley Kelly he replied, "Sure, birth date and address." They learned the address was always the same and that Charley always picked up the tab. He gave the detectives more than ten names of those recently tattooed for Charley Kelly.

Clifford and Flavin talked with the insurance investigator about what they learned from the tattoo artist. "What were you so anxious to talk to Charley Kelly about?" they asked.

"A $900.00 insurance policy he had on his brother, the prize fighter," he replied. "You see, a third party showed as beneficiary and collected $825.00 which had been assigned to him as security on money he loaned Cyclone. You just want to know the details," answered Clifford. "It makes no sense why anyone would let a north side derelict borrow that much money."

"There is something wrong," said the insurance man. "My firm can't make a move until we are sure of all the facts."

"Who is the man who loaned Cyclone such a roll?" asked Flavin.

"A dry cleaner by the name of Ernest," Bill the insurance investigator said.

"Charles D. Ernest of 2819 East Ninth Street?" Flavin inquired.

"Yes," Bill answered.

The two detectives felt the heat of excitement as they began to gain ground at last, even though they weren't sure how. They knew they needed to concentrate more on the strange cleaning man who bought booze for the north side floaters and later had them tattooed. However, they lacked enough evidence to bring him into the station for questioning. During their investigation, they learned something of his background. He migrated from Germany and became a naturalized citizen. He was 43 years old and came to Kansas City by way of Nashville, Tennessee. After moving to

Kansas City, Ernest worked as an insurance salesman for a short time, and then studied as a law student.

Armed with this information, they met again with their friend in the insurance business. They learned from him that Ernest bought several policies on several people. Most of the people were skid row bums, but among the names of those insured was Jerry Flaherty. Mr. Flaherty turned out to be an employee of a cleaning firm in direct competition with Ernest. He lived with his wife in a small hotel on Independence Avenue. The detective team immediately went there to question him about Ernest.

They soon learned that Flaherty was acquainted with Ernest and had received a beating at his hands a short time before. Flaherty had been subpoenaed to testify for an insurance company in a case involving Ernest. Mr. Ernest also threatened Flaherty and scared him into leaving Kansas City. Flaherty told the detectives that he had been with Ernest when he gave a pint of derail to Cyclone. He had doped the derail with two white pills. Flaherty had been informed that Cyclone died later. Flaherty also related to the detectives how Ernest attempted to get extremely friendly with him. He tried to persuade Flaherty to take out an insurance policy on his mother-in-law. When he refused, Ernest ordered him to leave Kansas City.

Clifford and Flavin gathered a lot of information but had no evidence strong enough to substantiate an arrest. The detective team took their story and information to Lt. Phil Hoyte, their commanding officer. He ordered them to stick with the assignment and work on nothing else until they cleared up this wholesale murder mystery.

They returned to the derelicts and began piecing the puzzle together. They found several who turned Ernest down on different deals to mark and insure them. They also talked to several men who had been approached by Ernest to do away with these marked men. The investigation became so involved it took more than a year to complete.

When the two officers finally presented the evidence for prosecution, they charged Ernest with first-degree murder, two charges of assault with intent to maim, and two charges of assault with intent to murder. Ernest was brought to trial on March 8, 1937. He was sentenced to the penitentiary in Jefferson City for twenty years.

These two officers went on to complete a long, interesting career before their retirement from the Kansas City Missouri Police Department.

FIRST TWO-WAY RADIO

IN SEPTEMBER 1935, police cars were first equipped with two-way communication. Five cars were equipped in the beginning, with one car added each day until a total of twelve were on the streets. On the evening of September 17, 1935, Lt. Roy DeShaffon cruised the streets of Kansas City, extending his tour deep into Jackson County, while maintaining two-way communication with the Police Dispatcher at Headquarters.

Starting at Eighteenth Street and Grand Avenue, car number 132 drove to Twelfth Street on Grand where he executed a left turn. He continued east on Twelfth Street to Van Brunt Boulevard, north on Van Brunt to Independence Avenue, and into the Sheffield district. There he turned into Blue Ridge Extension. He then returned to Eighteenth Street and Grand Avenue by way of Fifteenth Street (Truman Road). At the beginning of the journey, one of the passengers flipped a switch and spoke into a small hand microphone, "Car number 132, now leaving Eighteenth and Grand Avenue."

Immediately from the Police Dispatcher at Headquarters came the reply over Police Radio Station KGPE, "Okay, Car 132, at Eighteenth and Grand." So it was for the entire trip. He made contact with Headquarters at frequent intervals. Each time the dispatcher's reply came back quickly, clearly, and crisply. "Car 132 now traveling south on Blue Ridge Extension," said the officer in the cruiser. "O.K., Number 132 on Blue Ridge Extension," came back a snappy reply from the dispatcher, located approximately twelve miles from the speeding test car.

The value of the two-way communication quickly became apparent. Although cruisers and patrol vehicles had been able to receive instructions from a dispatcher, their only means of conveying their location and other important information had been by telephone, which frequently meant loss of valuable time. With the addition of cars with transmitting stations, patrolmen and detectives were able to keep the dispatcher informed of their whereabouts. This gave the dispatcher the capability to mobilize as many cars as necessary to take part in a car chase or other emergencies. Should an officer be pursuing a felon or a carload of desperadoes, he immediately notified the dispatcher of his location and circumstances. The dispatcher, in turn, communicated with other cars to set up a roadblock, intercept the suspect, and prevent his escape.

In 1935, there were two receiving stations in operation. They were set up to receive transmissions from moving cars. One was located on top of the courthouse, another on top of the National Bellas Hess Building at 5401 Independence Avenue. From these strategic locations, messages were relayed by direct wire to the dispatchers at Police Headquarters and to the transmitting equipment of the Police Radio Station, KGPE, located at the Twentieth and Flora Avenue Police Station. Two other receiving stations were later added a short distance south of Paseo High School.

Seventy officers completed a course in laws governing the use of radio. Each received a third class radio operator's license. Other men trained later and passed the examination to acquire their licenses. Each police vehicle was a mobile transmitter and receiver. Each unit was assigned regular call letters as an independent station. For ease in operation, the officers identified themselves on the air to the dispatcher by their car numbers.

In 1935, this equipment was considered the latest and

most sophisticated means of communication for emergency agencies such as metropolitan police departments. In a comparison with modern day communications systems, we must admit these early methods would prove primitive.

MOVING

ON NOVEMBER 19, 1938, the police department spent its last day of operation at Fourth and Main Streets, their home of forty-plus years. They were moving to the new building at 1125 Locust Street. This new building was to be known as the Municipal Courts Police Building. It was boasted that this would be the most modern police building, equipped with the most scientific devices, to combat crime in the United States.

Figure 112 — Old Police Building, Fourth and Main
Photo: Hugh Chase Private Collection

A citizen making a tour of the new building was overheard to remark, "The wages of sin in Kansas City will be paid from now on amid splendor." People were convinced that, indeed, the police department had moved uptown. The booking desk was located on the first floor with two offices at the end of the desk. At the end of the softly lighted lobby were two elevators with operators who asked, "Floor please." On the third floor was the magnificent office of the Police Director. New desks, gleaming typewriters and the latest filing equipment filled this anteroom.

The "show-up" room resembled a small theater. Equipment in the laboratory and photographic units impressed everyone with their array of shining machines. The iron bars in the jail remained in the background, never unpleasantly emphasized. A spacious room housed the dispatcher's office, equipped with streamlined equipment and two busy dispatchers with their eyes on an electronic map showing police cruiser's locations.

Figure 113
Police Headquarters Building
1125 Locust Street
Photo: Hugh Chase Private Library

Figure 114
Chief Robert J. Coffee
April 1939-July 1939
Hugh Chase
Private Collection

A nineteen-year-old man, arrested shortly after seven o'clock while attempting to rob a drugstore at Fourteenth and Grand, was the first prisoner booked into the new quarters. The first juvenile case placed on the records in the new building involved two thirteen-year-old boys. They were apprehended at Cliff Drive and Pendleton after they shot out thirty-six streetlights with an air rifle.

This new building was hailed as being the most modern police building in the United States. Today it is a landmark in Kansas City, Missouri.

CHIEF LEAR B. REED

CHIEF LEAR B. REED had been a Special Agent of the Federal Bureau of Investigation for sixteen years prior to becoming the twenty-sixth Chief of Police of the Kansas City Missouri Police Department. He was appointed Chief on July 11, 1939. He stepped into the most important changes in the history of the Police Department. Along with a new Board of Police Commissioners appointed by the Governor of the State of Missouri, he brought the Police Department out of the jaws of corruption into a new, progressive, and efficient law enforcement organization. Prior to passage of the "State Police Law" in 1939, a dark cloud of corruption known as "Home Rule" hung over the Kansas City Police Department.

The political machine submerged Kansas City into a widespread mire of corruption. This cancer reached into all branches of City and County Government, and resulted in a scandal, which smeared the city's reputation everywhere. The army of parasites attached to the machine did its dirty work for the crumbs thrown their way. The machine's stock-in-trade was the corruption of many people, in and out of public office. By the end of 1937 and early 1938, the degradation reached a point where the day of reckoning could no longer wait.

Election of a clean-up administration, which overthrew the "McElroy regime" in City Hall, made more history. Corruption was on the way out, and the passage of the "State Police Law" in the spring of 1939 returned police control to the governor. This paved the way for the difficult task of bringing law enforcement back to Kansas City.

The Eighteenth Amendment to the Federal Constitution and the Volstead Act did more to make crime a business than any other curse this country ever suffered. It brought into existence the worst gangs ever known. It caused more corruption in high places than anything else did. It resulted in more killings than any other time. Nothing has ever resulted in as much graft in law enforcement. No other single thing ever poured as much cash into the coffers of gangdom. The attempt to enforce it brought forth a horde of incompetent, insincere, untrained, and uncontrolled men in many places. The "alky" racket led to a far more flagrant and widespread traffic in narcotics. The Prohibition Era taught the underworld what it did not already know about organizing and operating as a business. The outlaw army of the land wanted prohibition to remain. The Repeal of the Eighteenth Amendment meant the loss of the most lucrative source of money crime had ever known. With the repeal and the Volstead Act, the underworld had to look to other fields. Bank robberies increased and bond thefts and jewelry robberies jumped to an all time high. Huge swindles in stocks, oil royalties, and other fields developed into an epidemic. Prostitution and gambling were organized on a big scale. Various organizations put the bite on legitimate business. As legitimate business bowed and appeased, the squeeze by gangsters got worse. Gangs took over in the ranks of labor, and business kept bowing and appeasing. Thus, the labor racketeers came into being. We found this land of the free and home of the brave infested with crime, labor racketeers, and filthy politics.

Chief of Police Reed penned the following in September of 1941 in his book, *Human Wolves:*

"The Bowery, the Barbary Coast, Chinatown, the Orient, Singapore and other notorious spots on the globe that have been in the spotlight of fact as fancy — none of them had

anything on Kansas City, the 'Heart of America,' the city of beautiful homes, parks and boulevards, the 'Gateway to the Southwest.'

Exaggeration? Don't you believe it! I know whereof I speak. I saw it and dealt with it.

We found the opium pipe in full glow. Walk in, pay the price, hit the pill, float off into that land of daisies not within the category of old Morpheus, awake, and depart! No questions asked! Little girls visiting the quarters of men, of different colors, for ten cents, some gum drops or a bottle of pop. Narcotics selling at underworld par as freely as apples and peanuts. Sex perversion more rampant than the wildest imagination could conceive.

Little boys stealing, individually and in gangs, in the style of filching Gypsies. Crooked gambling flourishing (sub-rosa) even after a grand jury had dealt it a severe blow.

Confidence men walking the streets as freely as honest merchants and plying their trade unmolested. The town divided into two districts with an overlord in charge of each district, 'exclusive territory' not to be invaded by the gang working the other. A huge take, a generous split of which found its way in the pockets of the venal politicians.

Girls of the scarlet profession came from all directions to the town where they could get protection, plied their trade openly in the downtown district, and harbored bank robbers, thieves, narcotic peddlers, and other criminals. They had been told not to leave town, that no Chief of Police could run them out.

Corruption was not confined to the underworld, venal politicians and crooked policemen. Many men and women of reputed respectability dipped into the mire from time to time, satisfying a craving for a thrill or yielding to a weakness."

Corruption, the gigantic underworld octopus, reached its tentacles into business, public office, law enforcement, and even the privacy of the home. It forced Policemen to: live where they were told, vote the way they were told, deliver

Figure 115 — Tom Pendergast (3rd from left) and unidentified men — City Control (Home Rule)
Hugh Chase Private Library

an allotted number of votes on election day to hold their jobs, give up half their salaries in the form of lugs and cuts to satisfy the greed of the machine, and close their eyes to vice, filth, and crime because it was operating the political machine. They were fired if they tried to do an honest job of law enforcement. This was the status of your Police Department during "home rule."

Dynamite was placed in buildings owned by businessmen who refused to bow to the will of the underworld gangsters. These scare tactics were the forerunner of a reign of terror in 1938, when vandals roved the city, wrecking building fronts, damaging interiors, destroying equipment and stacks of merchandise with bombs, smashing plate glass windows, and defying the police to act. The gangsters had numerous lawyers on their payroll to spring any who happened to be arrested by an honest Police Officer courageous enough to do his duty!

Under the corrupt regime, certain people were carefully indexed. Police officers knew these people were not to be arrested under any circumstances — including homicide. Traffic tickets were not to be issued to vehicles parked on a city street with a red ribbon or bandanna tied around the steering column. This was a courtesy to the North Side Democratic Club, which was loaded with gangsters. If an officer made the mistake of ticketing one of these vehicles, he lost his job or worse. Fixing traffic tickets was the rule and not the exception. A Police Lieutenant at the booking desk had the specific job of insuring that no criminal who was "right" with the machine got behind bars. If an officer was aggressive enough to put a criminal in jail, there was a Lieutenant there to embarrass and belittle the officer in the presence of prisoners and bystanders for their "boners."

In Kansas City, Missouri, it was apparent that some labor leaders had ceased to function as law-abiding representatives and had degenerated into gangs of racketeers who stopped at nothing to force their will upon the citizens of the community. From the 1920's through the 1940's, the city and ranks of labor suffered a vicious racketeering force of criminals and hoodlums. The racketeering foisted upon labor and the community started in 1917. That year, John Lazia, bank robber and petty hoodlum, was sentenced to fourteen years in the penitentiary for robbery. He served only eight months of that term and was released. He returned to Kansas City and called himself a politician. It is still not known how Lazia got his early release from prison.

John Lazia controlled some slot machines, a few prostitutes, and some votes. During a municipal election armed thugs beat, kidnapped, and murdered members of the opposition at Lazia's direction. This established him as an enforcer within the political machine. Lazia truly became a power to be reckoned with. He appointed men to the Police Department and to other city, county, and state positions. John Lazia appointed the first Director of Police under the reign of terror gently called "home rule." During various sensational kidnapping investigations, Lazia sat in the office of the Director of Police and gave orders as to what should and should not be done. After becoming a political power, the ever-cunning Lazia got the idea that organized labor was a fertile field for racketeering. Money from the honest workers, paid into the organization's coffers, enabled him to buy a lakeside resort, to be flush at all times, and to be a big shot. The monthly dues, however, constituted only a small part of the "take" in his racket. Lazia's gang forced business concerns to accede to his demands. This made wonderful jobs for gunmen and hoodlums.

Lazia's first big venture into the field of labor was the organization of the Cleaners and Dyers. He imported underworld characters from St. Louis, Missouri and Chicago, Illinois. These men blew up cleaning and dyeing shops, brutally beat employees, and forced businessmen to raise prices. The take for Lazia was tremendous.

Lazia's influence was not confined strictly to this organization. Because of his political position and influence with Police and other organizations, he was able to dictate policies to certain labor leaders. Kansas City was in the grip of gangsters.

Certain groups became envious of Lazia's tremendous financial return and attempted to "muscle in." Lazia ran his competitors out of town using his political position and connection to the police. Because of this, the gang that coveted Lazia's power set out to eliminate him.

John Lazia was shot to death while parking his vehicle at 2:40 a.m., July 10, 1934. Not long after his death the Boss of the political machine, Tom Pendergast, placed another gangster in Lazia's chair. Some say it was less than ten minutes after learning of his death.

Chief Reed had his work cut out as he was sworn in as the new Police Chief under State Control. Shortly after becoming Chief, he set out to close down the gangster elements and the sources of their money. Numerous attempts were made on his life. The underworld tried to set him up on frames with prostitutes and payoffs— to no avail. Chief Reed remained steadfast in his course to clean up Kansas City and the gangsters. Even with State control of the Police Department, Chief Reed dealt with ruminants of the political machine at every turn. In order to fight crime and win, he examined his new police department. What the new Chief found in his internal investigation was, in his words, a "nightmare." The following are examples of what he recorded. These samples of corruption are picked at random to give the reader an idea of the kind of police department Kansas City had during the "home rule" period prior to July 11, 1939.

Radio supplies are very expensive and those used by the Police Department are purchased with public funds, money paid in the form of taxes. In one day, 270 radio tubes were taken from the police radio store and placed on private cars. At another time, ten radio sets were taken from the department. It was stated that they were placed in the cars of racketeers and hoodlums. There are no records to show if an investigation was made by the police to locate and recover all that expensive property, or to catch and prosecute the thieves.

One night a large tire shop in the south end of the city was reported burglarized. Later some of the stolen tires were found on the personally owned automobile of the radio dispatcher who received the complaint and dispatched the officers to the scene of the crime. There is no record that the dispatcher was reprimanded, prosecuted, or discharged.

A newspaper carrier observed two thieves attempting to break into a drug store. The carrier immediately notified the police, and three cars went to the location. The officers forced the carrier to leave, and then loaded the police cars with loot from the drug store. Same ending, no prosecutions, all hushed up!

A paint company on the west side was burglarized and a small quantity of paint stolen. Company officials made an examination and knew exactly how much paint was missing. Police Officers were assigned to make an investigation. After they finished their "investigation," the company had hardly any paint left. The owner of the store was a member of the American Legion. He made a strong complaint to a certain police lieutenant on the Kansas City police force, who was also a legionnaire and the missing paint was returned.

A well-known criminal wanted for bank robbery and murder, had been sought for sometime by honest law enforcement officers. It developed that a lieutenant on the Kansas City force, not the one connected with the paint deal, was meeting this criminal nearly every night in a dive on Twelfth Street and was protecting him and advising him how to evade the law.

A notorious gangster and racketeer, who for reasons better known to others had not been put out of circulation, got out of his usual field of criminal activities and found himself charged in a state warrant with rape. The warrant was not given to detectives who in the ordinary course of police work served such warrants. It was given to an employee who worked inside, which was unusual. The employee was the relative of a former Chief of Police. The employee served the warrant. The criminal had a large amount of money in his pocket. The criminal was not booked and the employee became a lot richer. A large detective who was for years a member of the Kansas City force had bragged one time to Chief Reed that he "made 'em talk," and that he never bruised his fists on anyone he wanted to make confess to a crime. This detective took his victims to isolated spots near the riverbank and "stomped their damn heads in." He laughed as he told of kicking men in the head and bursting their eardrums, how he put his shoe heel in their eyeballs and otherwise persuaded them to "voluntary" confessions.

This representative of law enforcement, with a huge body and very small brain, operated a cheap, filthy hotel in the downtown district, where Tom and Bill McMullen, Charles

Enochs, Murray Gould, George Karatosis, Rolla Wade, Pat Pendleton, Otto Jackson, William Orr (alias Bill Grant), all notorious bank robbers, thieves, and racketeers, resided.

This hotel was connected with one directly south of it. The detective had made arrangements with the proprietor of the adjoining hostelry to permit his criminal guests to cross over a passageway into the second hotel in the event any officers came to the detective's hotel looking for any of them. On one occasion, one of these guests, who it was claimed killed a policeman during the hold-up of a shoe store, snatched a woman's purse in the heart of the business district and jumped into this detective's automobile and was driven away to safety. This was the detective who kicked confessions out of accused men.

Two police detectives learned through their investigations that Orr, alias Grant, had committed a series of cafeteria hold-ups. Orr was living at the hotel at the time. The officers could not apprehend Orr as long as the hotel-operating detective was around. They had to put an informant in the hotel to make arrangements and notify them. When the stage was set and the head-stomping detective was absent, the investigating officers arrested Mr. Orr, confronted him with the evidence, and he admitted having robbed the five leading cafeterias in the downtown district.

The detective who operated the hotel was so incensed because an arrest had been made in his hotel that he resigned his police job. The officers who made the arrest were severely reprimanded by a Chief of Police, who then re-employed the detective who had harbored the criminal.

The detectives who had made the arrest went back to the same hotel and found five fully loaded guns under the cushions on a divan in the front room. Undoubtedly, the guns were placed in readiness for the use of the outlaws in case honest officers come around when they were there. All of this was made known to a Chief of Police who did nothing about it. The hotel-operating detective, according to facts later de-

veloped during an investigation, drove a notorious robber out of town after robberies and on each ride got his split of the proceeds. The robber was, on each occasion, taken to a place where he could board a bus for Chicago.

Orr finally was sentenced to a term of ten years in the penitentiary, but served only a small part of the sentence. He was paroled to a certain police detective who, having been discharged from the present department, operates the same small hotel. Orr became his employee.

During Kansas City's reign of terror, the city was divided into the west side and the east side, for confidence racket purposes. The east side was controlled by one "Pappy," and the west side by one "Otto." Each maintained an office and did things in the style of a successful businessman. Confidence racket men desiring to do business in Kansas City had to see Pappy or Otto first. The jurisdictional line was finely drawn. There was no overlapping of territory, just as business maps out its sales territories.

The operations of these confidence men, which in the 1920's and 1930's cost the people of Kansas City hundreds of thousands of dollars, was not interfered with so long as this arrangement was not disturbed and the territorial confines were adhered to. The payoff was thirty per cent of the entire "take" paid to certain police officials.

The wife of a police officer had something to do with the hiring and placing of women who worked as detectives in downtown stores. During the fur sales each season, nationally known fur thieves came to Kansas City without apparent fear of molestation, and a large number of expensive furs were stolen or "boosted," in the language of the shoplifter, and sold in other cities.

It was confidentially related that some individuals connected with law enforcement received their "cut" regularly because of these operations.

Prostitutes beat a rhythm on the windowpanes from Twelfth to Eighteenth Streets and from Oak to the Paseo.

Nationally known writers described Kansas City as a "Cesspool of iniquity." The man who was in those days head of what should have been an important and effective detail in the police department was a close friend and protégé of the Chief of Police and the notorious Vice lord Carolla. The Chief of Police and the head of the Vice Detail split ninety-eight thousand dollars to look the other way and take no action.

During one of Kansas City's jubilant periods, shortly before the change from "home rule" to State control of the Police Department, a man operated a concession known as the "Holy City." He left the sanctuary of his concession and visited an assignment house operated by one Locke, a notorious Kansas City character. During the night, the operator of "Holy City" was robbed of $4,600.00. He reported the theft to the police department and the head of the police detail above referred to, was notified of the loss.

Within an hour, this police official met Locke in front of a designated restaurant, where they split the $4,600.00, each taking $2,300.00. Two plainclothes policemen learned of the shakedown and they immediately arrested Mr. Locke and made him split the $2,300.00 with them. Two other police officers who were detectives learned of this gravy train, so they then arrested Locke and made him split the $1,200.00, with $600.00 as their end. By that time, Locke caught on, ran to an automobile dealer, and paid the remaining $600.00 on a new car. The boys did not take the car, probably because it was too easily identified. It's a wonder they didn't steal the "Holy City."

A bank robber, being sought by Federal Law, came to Kansas City and went to a house of prostitution. During the night, the prostitutes stole $6,000.00 and a .45 caliber automatic pistol from the robber. He was in no position to seek police aid, so he left town without a squawk. The prostitutes went on a spending spree with the bankroll. They hired a taxicab and went to Omaha, Nebraska — quite a taxi ride for the girls.

The same police officials who took the first cut of the $4,600.00, got wind of the bank robber-prostitute deal, and went to Nebraska, where he arrested the girls. He brought them back to Kansas City, split the money, and released them. A dope-peddler and underworld character operated the house of prostitution by the name of Lamonti.

Mildred and Billie were sisters who operated a house of prostitution on Holmes Street. Billie claimed the affections of one Pretty Boy Floyd. These women specialized in getting very young girls to "work" in their place. They drove along the highways, located young girl hitchhikers, and inveigled them into lives of debauchery. On one occasion, two girls, one thirteen and the other fourteen, were found in this house badly infected with a social disease. Mildred and Billie were careful not to cross a state line, or cause the transportation of any girl across a state line, for immoral purposes. They did not want any trouble in Uncle Sam's Court.

The police official referred to in the $4,600.00 and $6,000.00 shakedowns, gave Mildred and Billie protection. The girls had two brothers who objected to Billie keeping company with Pretty Boy Floyd. Their dead bodies were found, one in Kansas City, Kansas and the other behind a billboard at Fourteenth and Charlotte in Kansas City, Missouri.

The most efficiently operated strumpet establishment in Kansas City at that time was located in the 1100 block on Cherry Street. Nell was its mistress. Nell was so friendly with the police she adopted their schedule. The girls worked "police shifts." One group was on duty from 8:00 a.m. to 4:00 p.m. Still another and larger crew took care of the rush period from 4:00 p.m. until midnight. Another worked from 8:00 p.m. until 4:00 a.m. and still another from midnight until 8:00 a.m. They guaranteed at least sixteen girls on duty at all times. Courtesy and politeness was assured all customers. Adequate protection, certainly not without compensation, was given Nell's place at all times by the police officer referred to, on the personal orders of a Charles Carolla.

A railroad conductor objected to being robbed by prostitutes. In an argument with their pimp, something caused the conductor to fall down a long stairway. When the homicide detail from the police department arrived, the victim was dead. His head bore the appearance of having been slugged. A police sergeant who was known to be on the "take" announced that the deceased had died of "heart failure." No further investigation.

A secretary to a Chief of Police gave protection to a bawdy house across the street from a well-known hotel. His jurisdiction was absolute. His position would not permit any muscling in. A bossy little fellow, who served a long term for violation of the Federal Narcotic Laws, was the collection agent for the policemen who protected so many prostitutes. He was a city employee and authorized to carry a gun and have a siren on his automobile. He was very prominent in a certain north end political club.

On one of the city's principal boulevards, across the street from a large church, Belle, sister of a racketeer who was murdered at Sixth Street and Broadway, operated a house of prostitution. The same vice policeman listed earlier, a Chief of Police, and a secretary to a chief protected her. Another house of prostitution named Madge's Place on Charlotte Street received excellent protection from a Chief and his secretary. The most exclusive place of this time in the city was on the Paseo, next to a public park where residents of the community and many children gathered for play and recreation.

In the center of the downtown hotel district there were so many prostitutes gathered in the evening that others could hardly use the sidewalk. It was the practice of the girls to catch a "chump," take him to a room, and slip him a "Mickey Finn." On one occasion, a well-known streetwalker took a "chump" to a hotel room. The victim observed the girls' procurer, known as a "pimp," going through his clothes. He leaped to save his valuables. The prostitute ripped him with a finger-string knife. He was taken to the General Hospital and died. The sergeant in charge of the homicide detail said the man died from pneumonia.

Many bellhops and porters enticed young girls into the clutches of the prostitutes. These procurers received thirty percent of the girls' charges. From 1939 through 1941, during a shutdown period by police, it was discovered that many of the women were infected with syphilitic sores.

Kansas City was the clearing point for the narcotic rings during the 1930's. This racket in Kansas City was a stench in the nostrils of the nation. It was said that a justice of the peace handled these matters for the underworld. A representative of the police department was in the Federal Narcotic Bureau Offices and learned that the "Federals" were about to "knock off" a place. In a separate room, the government men listened over a telephone extension and heard the police officer call the justice of the peace referred to and inform him that the "Feds" were about to raid so and so place. To see if the tip-off actually worked, the narcotics agents waited a little while and then went to the joint and found everything, including the furniture, moved out.

Police officers assigned to the Narcotic detail in the police department (not all of them) were selected and okayed by the narcotic syndicate. Those who were not so selected had their hands tied. Millions of dollars worth of contraband narcotics were sold in Kansas City over a period of a few years without even a finger being raised. It is bad enough when politics interferes with or dominates law enforcement in any degree, but when politics makes a city safe for these fiends of hell to buy, sell, and transport narcotics, what decent argument can anyone make for the political machine in control? Even if we could overlook all the crookedness (ghost voting, job using, fixing, framing, lugging, country bookkeeping, numbskull prosecutors, "piano player arrangement," wholesale grand larceny in high places, and all the other phases of the fiasco of the Heart of America), no man or woman with a spark of decency or conscience could condone a politi-

cal outfit that not only permitted, but aided and abetted, the narcotic traffic.

On one occasion, some police detectives stopped a car to question the occupants. What a mistake these men, sworn to enforce the law, made. It was indeed embarrassing for them when they learned that John Picone was in that car. When the officers pulled alongside, one of the criminals in the car threw a package containing a large quantity of morphine cubes into a vacant lot. Picone boldly and indignantly made his identity known. What did these upstart policemen mean? Wasn't he protected? What the hell kind of a racket were the cops working anyway? He would take care of them in short order. Of course, the officers had families and jobs were scarce. Besides, to be fired over such a deal as this would mean a fellow would be out of luck in Jackson County. The strong arm of the law apologized in all humility. They went into the vacant lot and searched diligently until they located the package of morphine. They then returned it to Picone and worried for days about the security of their jobs.

During an investigation by Federal Agents of James Abbott, a notorious gangster, a detective sergeant of the police department pretended to aid the government agents. A female named Bertha was arrested in an effort to get closer to Abbott. The detective sergeant and Abbott had a telephone conversation, and the sergeant informed Abbott fully of the activities and knowledge of the government men. "How about the girl?" asked Abbott, and the sergeant answered, "I'll find out." The sergeant then called and conferred with the head of the narcotic detail in the police department. He then called Abbott again and told him to "lay off the girl, she is a stool pigeon for the government."

Federal Agents, accompanied by a ranking officer of the police department, hid in a storeroom on Fifteenth Street in an attempt to apprehend a notorious narcotics peddler. The police official had not been informed as to the identity of the man about to be apprehended. An informant was stationed across the street. Just before the criminal arrived, the federal agents told the police officer that "Smitty" would come by and meet the informant. The police official slipped into another room and called his wife. The criminal then drove up, beat the informant almost to death, and drove away. As the culprit did not make any delivery of dope, the federal men could not make an arrest. They drove to the police department, let the officer out, and went away. In a few minutes the federal officers drove to Smitty's house and found the police official there receiving his payoff. Would any higher-up cause the dismissal of such a police officer? No!

Officers of the Kansas City Police Department were used during the black days of our reign of terror to drive the cars of gangsters. Such additional protection was not necessary, but the boys wanted to be sure at times. Police officers serving as chauffeurs for dope peddlers may not impress you, if you read too rapidly. Stop and think about it. Narcotic peddlers are killers and their trade promotes all other types of major crime. Motorcycle officers were also used by the underworld to transport and deliver narcotics in Kansas City.

I recall a case in which a number of efficient and loyal investigators spent more than the average time and effort to develop the evidence and apprehend the guilty. The officers hid at Nineteenth and Oak Streets and waited for the delivery of the "hot stuff." The criminal ambled into sight. Two thieving policemen jumped from ambush, strong-armed him, and snatched him into darkness. They took the contraband and $100.00 from the violator. They went directly to a place operated by a notorious criminal and sold the contraband for a nice profit.

In many cases, it was necessary for federal agents to give money to informants to be used in purchasing narcotics from peddlers. Some police officers would "shake down" these informants and take the money away from them. It was necessary for the federal agents to force these policemen to return the money.

Certain officers of the Kansas City Police Department had a beautiful racket, which very few knew about. The protected peddlers always knew when an out-of-town peddler made a large purchase of dope. The local fellows would inform these police officers who would grab the out-of-town peddler, take the dope away from him, and return it to the man who sold it to the out-of-town peddler. For this racket, the police officers received a very worthwhile remuneration.

On one occasion, a pair of competent, honest detectives were the first to arrive at an address where a death had been reported. They found that a man had hanged himself and left a suicide note. Members of the homicide squad arrived, looked over the scene, had a consultation with members of the family, and reported the cause of the man's death as accidental rather than suicidal. Questions that should have been asked but were not: How much did the insurance company pay? Was it true that some officers arranged such matters for a consideration? Did insurance companies pay great sums of money in additional claims?

In another case, a body was found on the tracks beneath one of the public viaducts. Four witnesses made statements that the deceased had deliberately climbed up on the railing three feet above the viaduct and jumped. The homicide detectives listed the death as accidental. Did the insurance company that paid double indemnity know the facts?

One Irvin was engaged in the narcotic racket in a city to the north of Kansas City. He came to Kansas City and fell in with a local underworld character who operated a nightclub where customers were "Mickey Finned," not far from Twelfth and Broadway. He became suspicious of Irvin and believed the latter to be a government informant. Irvin carried $5,000.00 and wore a diamond ring valued at $1,500.00. The underworld character had a shoplifting gang. The members were in jail in Oklahoma City, and $1,800.00 was needed to get them out on bail. A police radio message went out over the air that a man had been killed at St. John and Brooklyn *fitting Irvin's description. Five pairs of detectives rushed to the scene and arrived before the cruiser carrying the uniform officers. The detectives engaged in a free-for-all battle in an attempt to obtain the money and the diamond ring. Several detectives were kicked in the face and otherwise bruised and beaten. Neither the ring nor the money has ever been accounted for.*

Jamie was a bad one. In addition to her own brilliant scheming and smoothness, she had the god of luck and the finest police protection on her side. She got by for a long time. It seemed that those strong arms of the law who were so interested in Jamie's welfare had determined that nothing would cause her downfall. No man would put a crimp, at least a permanent one, in her narcotic racket. Two uniformed police officers, not familiar with the slimy trails of the dope reptiles and not sufficiently "in the know," arrested Jamie. They obtained, incidental to the arrest, a large quantity of morphine sulfate. A serious mistake had been made. Another blunder on the part of "harness bulls" who had not been posted and had not taken the trouble, as all patrolmen in those days should have done, to find out whom they could arrest and whom they could not. There was consternation in the household. Something had to be done. Such nerve, such effrontery, arresting Jamie! What were things coming to, anyway? An officer might as well say something naughty about the North Side Democratic Club and desecrate the name of John Lazia. Jamie was in jail, her name was on the book, and the morphine was in the property room. Now the fix had to look at least half-way genuine. The head of the narcotic detail in the police department had been appointed by the bigwig in the North Side Club. They had a conference. The sleuth went to the property room and got the package of dope, took it, along with Jamie, "to charge her before the U.S. Commissioners." Jamie and the sleuth never reached the Commissioners office. The sleuth announced that the patrolmen had made a serious mistake; the package contained milk of magnesia, not morphine, and proved his contention by quickly eating a white tablet, and quickly getting Jamie and her valuable package out of the police station. This, dear reader, was known as the "switch." Jamie went on her way with her morphine. Those present at the time and familiar with the case stated that the police officer received a roll of bills from Jamie.

A small factory in Kansas City was blown up one night. A few minutes later, a well-known police detective crashed his automobile not far from the explosion. The police car was wrecked. It was not reported that the detective was making his escape after having blown up the factory.

During a strike of beauty parlor operators, high sounding and extravagant statements were made as to what investigation the police were making and what results could be expected. Many windows were being smashed and wholesale

Figure 116 — Election Day Murders, March 27, 1934
"Open War at the Polls" declares Kansas City Times, October 20, 1966
Hugh Chase Private Library.

damage was being done. Of course, it would not have done any good to suggest to the police that a detective, a very close relative of a Chief of Police, be arrested as the leading strong-arm man in the property wrecking campaign then going full blast. Nor would any purpose have been served by demanding that another detective, whose wife then operated a beauty parlor, be jailed and charged as one of the ringleaders in this episode.

Chief Reed left the Kansas City Police Department after almost three years of fighting and cleaning up the corruptive areas of the Department. He later wrote that he thought the police department, after being purged of the criminal elements, was one of the finest and most progressive in the United States. Chief Reed, upon leaving the police department, entered into private industry in California.

Figure 117
Sergeants and Patrolmen's badges under Reed's Tenure (City Control)
Photo: Hugh Chase Private Library

RESERVES

THE AUXILIARY POLICE began early in 1942, shortly after the declaration of World War II. They felt that modern transportation made Kansas City much closer to the actual fighting, and they needed a secondary line of defense in the event of an emergency. Training classes opened at police headquarters for 1,350 volunteers. They received their training under the supervision of Superintendent Lou Smyth. The training classes started with thirty-hour basic and advanced courses in first aid and fifty hours riding in a police car observing field duties. Courses in firearms and jujitsu were given in regular weekly drills following the initial training. Upon completion of this training, the men were assigned to police department duty.

These officers soon began paying dividends to the citizens. An incident, which occurred on October 30, 1942, proved this point. James McLeese (one of the officers), was waiting in the Traffic Bureau for his evening assignment and hoping for some excitement. This particular event turned out to be a bad one. A hit-and-run driver struck and killed a fifty-one year old man who was attempting to board a streetcar at Twenty-Second and Troost Avenue.

A witness got the first three numbers of the license plate. The car sped by so quickly that he was unable to get the last three numbers. Investigating officer, Alex Schwendt, picked up the dead man's hat and scooped up bits and pieces of broken headlight glass. Officer Schwendt placed these fragments of glass on a desk in the traffic and safety office. Auxiliary Officer James McLeese asked if he could look at the bits of glass. The investigating officer nodded approval. McLeese put the glass together to spell a word "multi beam" and the word "Guild" as well as a serial number.

This meant that the headlight came from one of four makes of automobiles produced by General Motors Corporation during certain years. Armed with this information and a piece of missing chrome, Lieutenant Mahoney from the traffic bureau took to the streets in search of the car.

He found a 1937 Oldsmobile matching his evidence at the southwest corner of Twelfth and Oak Streets. Mahoney returned to the office and asked McLeese to check the location of all 1937 Oldsmobiles in the vicinity at the time the accident occurred. McLeese soon came up with answers. Thirty minutes after midnight, members of the Missouri State Highway Patrol arrested the owner and driver of the car at his home in Hickman Mills.

This group of men worked as an auxiliary unit until September 1953. At that time, an amendment was made to establish the auxiliary police unit as a police reserve unit. This brought the reserve officers under the same law that governed the officers of the Kansas City Police Department. This action gave the reserve officer the same privileges and authority as a regular officer. These men give their time without pay, and serve in any capacity or unit in which they draw their assignment. They have handled the parking and patrolling of Swope Park during Starlight Theater season since opening day. Reserve officers work at ballparks, high school activities, the Mayor's Christmas parties for the needy, events at the Municipal Auditorium, or any other event in the city where they are needed. They have served with honor in the day-to-day operation of the police department, often without recognition. Reserve Officer Russel Beckman was shot in the chest while checking some suspicious men at Thirty-Fourth and Indiana. On at least three occasions when regular officers were shot and wounded, the reserve officers either shot or apprehended the felons involved.

Many times these men are commended by the citizens for the professional manner in which they handle themselves and the situations they are called to handle. Individual reserve officers have received many awards. Some of the highest awards of valor have been awarded to the Reserve Officers of the Kansas City Missouri Police Department. Should there be one unit of the police department that deserves the title of hard-working and unsung hero, it would be for past, present and future members of the Police Reserves.

POLICE V.F.W. POST

V.F.W. POST # 9762 does an outstanding job of representing the Veteran's of Foreign Wars. Its membership is made entirely of officers or retired officers of the Kansas City Missouri Police Department. They are at the present time the only post in the State of Missouri that can boast this distinction.

At the close of World War II, when most veterans had taken their place in civilian life, many of them joined the

Figure 118 — The Informant November 1971

Figure 119 — The Informant November 1971

V.F.W. Russell M. (Roxie) Clough at that time belonged to Post # 18. Roxie was assisting in collecting dues from approximately eighteen members of the Police Department who held membership cards in V.F.W. Post # 18. While acting in this capacity and talking with the men, he found that due to the duties of the police department, they were unable to attend meetings and take an active part in the functions of Post # 18.

Someone suggested that a Post should be established made up only of law enforcement members. It would give officers more opportunity to take an active part and develop a feeling of camaraderie. With these two ideas, Roxie started inquiries toward the achievement of this goal.

He initially contacted his superiors in the Veteran of Foreign Wars. He asked about the feasibility of the idea and their sanction. They quickly informed him that they had no objections. They bought the idea and promised their help.

He then presented this idea to the Board of Police Commissioners. They not only gave their approval but volunteered space in the headquarters building to hold meetings temporarily. They also volunteered any assistance needed to establish the post.

An announcement was made of the intention to establish such a post. An organizational meeting was held on the fourth floor of headquarters building at 1125 Locust. The first three meetings convened in a small room located at the northeast corner of headquarters. More than seventy officers attended each of those first three meetings. They seemed to be off to a very good start.

The post was installed March 18, 1948. The ceremonies of installation for the new Post and the swearing in of new officers by Herb Chrisco and Willis B. McCulla took place on March 14, 1948. The officers elected to head the new Police Post # 9763 were:

Commander—Russel M. Clough
Senior Vice Commander—Loren Samples
Junior Vice Commander—Elmer Murphy
Quartermaster—James Newman
Chaplain—Harry Hogue
Advocate—Louis Davidson
Surgeon—Malcolm England
Adjutant—Kenneth Phillips
Officer of the Day—Harry Brashier
Bugler—Jack Hedrick
Trustee—John J. Rowland
Trustee—Wayne L. Misher
Trustee—Dale F. Hadley

The Post received their colors shortly after inception. Jaccards Jewelry Company, Goldman Jewelry Company, and Helzberg Jewelry Company purchased the flag for the Post. Each of these companies sent representatives to present these colors to the Post at an official ceremony. This ceremony gave birth to the idea of the "Police Color Guard."

The Board of Police Commissioners soon gave their permission for the members of the Color Guard to wear the regulation uniform with their V.F.W. hat for any official function. Since their establishment, V.F.W. Post # 9762 has furnished the color guard at the funeral of every police officer.

This Post has been represented in many parades in Kansas City and other communities. They have marched in every American Royal since the Post was founded. Each member shows a dedication to his Post, the police department, and his fellow man. In many instances, they have given both financial and other types of aid to citizens. Many people received aid without knowing who extended the helping hand.

The police V.F.W. Post # 9762 had many members who have gone on to higher offices in the V.F.W. Among them were:

Three all State Commanders—

Lee Coleman
Wilfred Brown
Jack Maxwell

Two Jackson County Council Commanders

Norman O'Hara
William Hutcherson

James Newman held the post of Jackson County Adjunct Quartermaster. Kenneth Brassfield and Kenneth Regnier have been Fourth District Commanders. In addition to those offices, William Hutcherson and Floyd Brassfield were both Commanders to the Order of Military Coolies. There are many more to name if space and time allowed.

These men have shown that they were all outstanding by their deeds and actions. They were gifted not only by bringing pride to themselves and members of the V.F.W., but also by association to the police department. The next time you witness this color guard or any other part of this V.F.W. Post, let them know your pride in them. Say, "Thank You."

GLEE CLUB

IN THE LATTER PART of January 1954, Chief Bernard C. Brannon issued a department memorandum approving the formation of a police glee club under professional direction. He pointed out that formerly the department had glee clubs, quartets, and a band. He directed officers interested in joining the chorus to contact Major Lou Smyth, director of Public Information.

Within a few days, five officers applied for membership in the chorus and by the end of February, enrollment closed with thirty voices. During February and early- March, auditions were held at police headquarters. On March 13 the police bulletin (an in-house publication) announced the first

Figure 120 — Metropolitan Police Band — 1923
Hugh Chase Private Library

rehearsal would be held on March 15 with Dr. W. Everett Hendricks directing. Dr. Hendricks was Associate Professor of Music at the University of Kansas City and a member of the Police Reserve Unit.

Dr. Hendricks arranged for weekly rehearsals in the auditorium of the American Legion World War II Memorial Building. He faced many difficulties in training the police chorus. It was impossible to have full attendance at any practice session due to shift changes, court appearances, days off, vacations, and illness.

The glee club made its first public appearance on April 28, 1954. The Kansas City Junior Safety Council held a meeting and luncheon in the World War II Memorial Building on the same day the chorus rehearsed. During the luncheon, the glee club sang three numbers to entertain the young people. This appearance created new problems for the police department. Invitations began coming from various organizations requesting the appearance of the glee club. Many invitations were declined due to the members' duty responsibilities. The second public appearance was before a meeting of the Kansas Peace Officer Association at the Town House Hotel in Kansas City, Kansas. Peace officers from all over the state had assembled there for a semi-annual conference.

The graduation ceremonies of the 43rd recruit class of the Kansas City Police Academy were held at the Playhouse of the University of Kansas City on May 20. The members of the chorus were seated at the right of the stage, facing the new policemen on the left. Members of the Board of Police Commissioners, Chief Brannon, and others were seated in the center of the stage. The chorus sang several numbers during the program, closing with a benediction, "The Lord's Prayer," sung by Jim Peterson and accompanied by the chorus. The public had been invited to attend the ceremonies. Once again, many invitations for other public appearances were received but could not be fulfilled.

Figure 121 — Kansas City, Missouri Police Band — 1940
Hugh Chase Private Library

A big event each year for police employees and their families was the police picnic given by the Board of Police Commissioners and Chief Brannon at Kansas City's beautiful Swope Park. Attendance usually ran close to 4,000. The Board invited many civic leaders and their families to join the police in their annual celebration held September 8, 1954. The police chorus was the featured entertainment. Dr. Hendricks produced old time police coats and helmets, obtained some mustaches, and developed ten comedy singers as a special feature. This was a huge success, and once again the Glee Club was flooded with invitations.

Graduation ceremonies of the 44th recruit class were held at the KMBC-TV Playhouse and again the public responded, filling the large auditorium. The chorus was once again a featured attraction. Roy E. Wike, Executive Secretary of the International Association of Police, extended an invitation to the chorus to sing at the opening session of the 61st annual conference of the Association in New Orleans on Mon-

Figure 122 — Unidentified members of Kansas City, Missouri Police Band at Pla-mor
Hugh Chase Private Library

day, September 27. Police funds could not be used to defray the expense of the trip, so a limited group of prominent Kansas Citians was invited to contribute the necessary funds. They met the sum needed within three hours. Chief Brannon, along with three members of the Board of Police Commissioners and their wives, attended the conference.

The Kansas City "Southern Belle" had to attach a special car for the members of the chorus. The train reached Baton Rouge, La., shortly after daylight on September 26. The Mayor, Chief of Police, Sheriff, a delegation of citizens, and a band greeted the singing officers at the railroad station. The chorus members left their car, lined up on the station platform, and burst into song. They sang several numbers for the welcoming delegation. Officials of the International Association of Chiefs of Police and a reception committee of young ladies in beautiful pastel costumes met the chorus in New Orleans. The chorus immediately lined up and sang to the beautiful southern belles, stopping all action at the big station until they loaded into waiting cars driven by state police. When the police conference opened on Monday morning, Chief Brannon presented the chorus to the crowded ballroom of the Hotel Roosevelt and Dr. Hendricks directed the singing of three numbers and several encores.

That evening, the chorus appeared at Ponchetrain Beach, where visiting police executives and their families enjoyed a fish dinner. Dr. Hendricks again used his comedy singers in their fantastic costumes. The 1,800 people in attendance responded with a continuous burst of applause.

The next public appearance occurred Sunday morning, October 3, when Chief Brannon spoke at the meeting of the Business Men's Bible Class in Ivanhoe Temple. During Christmas week, the chorus sang Christmas carols at Mercy Hospital, the Nettleton Home, and other institutions for or-

Figure 123 — Glee Club in Costume
The Informant April 1971

phans and the aged.

Despite the many difficulties of training and rehearsals, the police chorus gained recognition as an outstanding choral group in Kansas City and the national law enforcement field. The Glee Club became a piece of Kansas City history in 1959 as the demand for police service outgrew the available voice power. Sadly, the Kansas City Missouri Police Glee Club ended.

MONKEY

IT WAS A BEAUTIFUL AFTERNOON in the early fall of 1954. Officer Herman Spielberger had just taken over the responsibility of the district. He checked the police cruiser and pulled into Twelfth Street on the way to his assigned district. He started his watch and almost immediately was dispatched to the vicinity of Twentieth Street and Forest Avenue on an animal disturbance.

Upon arrival, officers from the city animal shelter met Officer Spielberger. He and the animal shelter employees spotted the animal at almost the same instant. A playful looking orangutan scampered across the tops of automobiles, through the treetops, and along the telephone and light wires strung along the streets.

Officer Spielberger stopped his police car. The monkey, instead of loping off through the trees as might be expected, came bounding into the police car with the officer. The monkey made a speedy entrance into the police car. With even greater speed, the officer made an exit.

In his explanation the officer said, "I have been called to handle opossums, cats, vicious dogs, and other animals, but never anything like this. When this creature jumped in the car and bared its teeth, I bailed out." Once in the car, the monkey quickly made himself at home. First, he dined on the officer's lunch, which he found handy in the front seat. After eating the last morsels of the sandwiches and cookies, he turned his attention to the car. He first checked the lights and other buttons on the dash and then put the car in gear.

While the monkey planned his trip, Officer Spielberger, Mr. Henry Jackson, and Mr. Roy E. Elb (concerned citizens attempting to assist the officer with the capture of the monkey), and employees of the municipal animal shelter held a meeting in the middle of the street to plan their strategy. They decided to attempt to entice him from the car into the street where they could slip a rope around his neck. Then they could easily bind him and place him in the animal shelter's wagon.

The men failed to give the monkey a script outlining the part he played in this drama. This was a grave mistake. The animal shot from the police car like a flash of light. He eluded his would-be captors and climbed to the top of a utility pole on the southwest corner of Twentieth and Forest Avenue. He perched atop the pole where he scratched and yawned in boredom. An estimated crowd of one hundred spectators gathered below to watch the free show.

Officer Spielberger went to the police cruiser and requested assistance over the radio. Sergeant Lawrence Gore responded. A short time later, Mr. George A. Beebe, supervisor from the animal shelter, arrived to offer assistance. He came armed with a lengthy pole with a noose attached.

Maneuvers soon switched from the ground to the air. Mr. Beebe raised the pole and attempted to slip the noose around the monkey's neck. The orangutan grabbed playfully at the noose. He tired of this game after a short time and swung from the pole to a tree and across another wire. Then he left the wire to jump into a tree growing in the front yard of 2100 Forest. Now the monkey decided to show his contempt for the public. He defecated onto his hands and heaved it towards the crowd. They quickly scattered.

The monkey went through these antics for another two hours as he outwitted every attempt at capture. The men became exhausted and decided to destroy the animal. That decision ended an eventful time with mixed emotions for all involved.

K-9 UNIT

IN 1956, THE CANINE PATROL was little more than an idea in the head of Captain Frank Daly. Captain Daly spent many hours and invested much physical effort investigating the use of dogs for police work.

The department first acquired Roger, a promising German Shepherd, from Springfield, Missouri. Roger appeared aggressive, healthy, and suitable for training. He met all requirements for the type of training and work expected of him.

Roger was assigned to work with Officer Edward Owens as his handler. As soon as possible, Roger and Ed were assigned to a foot beat in the area of the city market. They made an excellent showing, and the department soon saw the possibilities of a canine unit. They acquired three more police dogs.

They decided to expand the unit and sent four K-9 teams to the Police Department in St. Louis, Missouri where they received proper training. The four officers selected for this training were Ed Owens, Arthur Felts, David Spitcaufsky and Earl Davis. In June 1960, the four officers, with their four-footed partners, made the trip to St. Louis for a fourteen-week training course.

Upon their return to Kansas City, they found the police department hampered from a lack of funds. The four officers, in the initial phase of the unit, even paid for the animals' food from their own pockets. The program grew slowly through the struggles and efforts of these four officers. The unit's severely limited budget forced them to operate with a handicap. They needed kennels, training equipment, and a training area.

The city offered space at the municipal farm. Part of the area was covered in concrete for use as hog pens. The four officers constructed kennels and headquarters stretching nearly a city block. They worked on their off-duty hours and used materials donated by interested citizens. Kansas City became one of the premier training centers, providing training for the department's own canines and men, and training dogs belonging to other police agencies.

The animals were used initially in areas such as the city market and the ballparks. Their appearance greatly reduced armed robbery, purse snatches, and thefts. Crime in the city market virtually ended while a K-9 team worked that location.

Figure 124 — First four officers with their canine officers
Photo: Hugh Chase Private Library

The K-9 unit enjoyed outstanding success. Teams checked thousands of buildings, cars, and alleys every hour. The dogs tracked everything from peeping Toms to homicide suspects. Dogs are master trackers; they do not miss objects discarded or hidden by a suspect that human eyes might miss.

Men who work with the dogs and are involved in the program estimate that one dog equals ten men in crowd control. The men know that fifty percent of the effectiveness is psychological, due to fear of the animal. They also know that any action will be backed up when needed. A common misconception in the use of dogs is that they are trained killers. Nothing can be farther from the truth.

The history of the Canine Unit must include the mention of "Trooper." A tiny grave at the training center is a constant reminder of what their animals can mean to them. In the grave lies "Trooper." He was one of three dogs in the United States who gave their lives in the line of duty.

Trooper gave his life protecting Officer Scoville. Early one morning in 1961, they responded to a call to investigate a break in at Twenty-Seventh and Indiana. In a dark alley, two men jumped the officer, threw him to the ground, and started beating him. One swung a crowbar, which could have meant instant death to the policemen. Trooper lunged for the man's arm, but heavy clothing prevented a steady hold. Trooper struck repeatedly, grabbing at the man's face and pulling him backwards. His actions gave his handler a chance to pull his gun. He shot and killed one assailant. While this took place, the second suspect used the crowbar to strike a crippling blow across Trooper's back.

Officer Scoville received hospital treatment for his injuries. Trooper, crippled and in pain, went to the Police Veterinarian Hospital. All efforts to save the noble hero failed. Trooper, paralyzed and losing his battle with death, was put to sleep.

"Trooper" made the supreme sacrifice to protect and save his master. In September that same year, the Kansas City

The K-9 Corp Sign and their motto means just what they say!

Figure 125 — K-9 Corps Sign
The Informant July 1969

Missouri Police Department received the Golden Nyabone Award from the National Wayside Waifs, Inc. in recognition of "Trooper's" heroism.

Any of the animals now in the Canine Corps would react in the same manner should the situation arise. Officers in this unit have no way of knowing the number of times their four-footed partners have saved them from bodily harm, but they do praise their animals at every opportunity.

The next time you see an officer working with his canine companion, you will recognize an unbeatable team — the officer, one of the best trained and equipped in the nation, and his dog, a highly skilled and respected member of the police department.

HELICOPTER UNIT

THE KANSAS CITY POLICE DEPARTMENT was one of the first in a major city to use helicopter patrol. Their use has proved most helpful in apprehending criminals who have escaped or eluded officers.

Chief Bernard Brannon considered the feasibility of using the helicopter as a patrol vehicle as early as 1953. Their use was never attempted because of a shortage of money. Helicopter use was considered again in 1967. The International Association of Chiefs of Police (IACP) held its convention here in Kansas City. During the convention, the Hughes Tool Company displayed their ships and demonstrated them by making limited patrols over the city.

Police Chief Clarence Kelley showed a deep interest. He invited a representative of the Hughes Company to return to Kansas City for a ten-day trial period and a more complete evaluation. The results turned out to be most encouraging.

In November 1967, two officers from the Kansas City Police Department went to Lakewood, California to study their helicopter operation. Officer Bill Dycus and Captain Jack Brady made the study. These officers questioned citizens and businessmen of the community and found the use of helicopters to be a most favorable operation. Their report to the Board of Police Commissioners prompted the initiation of a similar program here.

In January 1968, plans were made to initiate this program. A unit commander and five officers were selected to

Figure 126 — Early helicopter
The Baton February 1959

begin training with an additional fifteen alternates.

The first six men went to Long Beach, California for training. Their training began April 1, 1968. "The World Associates" conducted these training classes. This firm specialized in training police officers to become helicopter pilots. After a six-week training test certification, they received a private helicopter license.

On May 10, 1968, the officers accepted delivery on three new model 300 helicopters at Palamar, California. From Palamar they flew the helicopters back to Kansas City.

Upon their return, these officers continued training until granted a commercial license with an instructor's rating. Six of the alternate officers began their training in September 1968.

These helicopters have proved useful in many phases of police work. They have been very effective when working with detectives on surveillances. They have been used to photograph crime scenes and to take photos for the health department in cases of pollution control. They have proved very useful in photographing riots and the following destruction. They are also used to follow vehicles that have run from the Police where pursuit by vehicle would endanger the public.

From its beginning, this unit received many citizen requests for various services. This lists only a few: search for a family pet, request to dry tennis courts, even a request to dry the playing field at Arrowhead Stadium. Once they received a request to search for a lost diaper bag.

On May 22, 1969 the unit received a call requesting them to rescue three men from a barge loaded with wheat about three hundred feet from shore near Wolcott, Kansas. The craft broke loose from its moorings and drifted downstream in the rapidly flowing Missouri River.

The call for assistance came in at 1930 hours in the afternoon. Sgt. James Lohmeyer and Sgt. William Moulder responded. They landed on the loose barge and brought the three men to safety. Many similar stories abound if time and space permitted.

The crime analysis section supplies information used to plan patrol duties and flight schedules. This allows them to evaluate and concentrate on areas that show a frequent recurrence of four major crimes: burglary, robbery, auto theft, and larceny.

Statistics of these crimes more than prove the value of these strange looking air-borne vehicles. Crime has shown a decrease up to twenty percent in areas patrolled by helicopters.

SLOT MACHINES

ON JULY 13, 1972, members of the vice squad recovered several coin operated machines, commonly known as slot machines, from a local warehouse. They received a telephone call from the manager stating they were holding the machines in storage. The manager told officers that according to police department tags attached, the machines appeared to have been seized from the Elk's Club at Seventh Street and Grand Avenue, on December 2, 1947.

Detectives Robert Carrington and John Dawson of the Vice and Gambling Unit responded to the warehouse. They met the manager who surrendered twenty coin-operated machines and miscellaneous parts. After recovering the machines, they were brought to police headquarters and placed in the property room.

These machines raised many questions. When did the police department first seize these gambling devices? What was the outcome of the cases involving them? What occurred to cause them to be stored in a local warehouse so many years? Research started with the hope that some of these questions could be answered.

On December 2, 1947, sixteen slot machines were taken in a raid from the Elk's Clubrooms, 120 West Seventh Street. Several of the machines still bore tags of the police department property room where they had been taken in earlier raids.

Sergeant Leroy C. Goodwin, of the inspection bureau,

followed the orders of Captain William Tobner. He gained admittance by following a late arriving member inside when a porter opened the clubroom door to admit this member. Most of the members attending the meeting were unaware of the raid.

Municipal Court Judge Earl Frost assessed a $1,000.00 fine against Clarence A. Perrine when he tried the case. Because of the raid the Elk's Club had their liquor license revoked on January 5, 1948.

Joseph N. Keirnan, director of city liquor control, pointed out at the hearing in March 1947, that Clarence A. Perrine, secretary of the lodge, and B. A. Babb, attorney for the organization, had signed an agreement. This agreement stated that any further gambling violations by the lodge would result in the revoking of the Elk's liquor license.

Joseph N. Minlace and Harry Whitney represented the lodge at the hearing. They contended that the slot machines were not on the premises as described in the liquor license granted to the club and that the machines were not being operated with the knowledge and consent of the lodge.

Sergeant Leroy Goodwin of the police department testified that he and L. C. Stolberg raided the Club after receiving an anonymous letter. Goodwin said the two officers entered the club with search warrants issued by Municipal Court Judge Earl Frost. The Sergeant said he went to the basement of the building and followed the corridor, which led to a door. He rapped on the door and a porter admitted him. "There were two members of the lodge playing twenty-five cent slot machines in the room, one of which was turned around facing the wall and not in operation."

The officers stated that beer and canned goods were stored in the room. They found several other slot machines behind a partition. Sergeant Goodwin testified that they sent for Perrine along with a photographer to take pictures of the illegal machines.

While they waited for the photographer, one of the Elk

members entered the room and put a quarter in the machine. The machine went through a gyration, tinkled, delayed, and then paid off six quarters. He then placed another quarter in the coin slot. This time after the gyrations ceased, a much louder jingle followed the delay, and the machine paid fourteen to one. At this point one of the officers identified himself and confiscated the money. He handed the Elk member his two quarters and placed the rest in an envelope to be introduced as evidence.

The machines contained money and were returned to the club after a replevin suit. The secretary declared that they did not wish to break the machines up because they were valued at $250.00 each.

The court ordered the slot machines returned to the Elk's Club. Evidently, all parties concerned forgot about them until the manager of the storage company discovered them twenty-five years later.

The slot machines were picked up from the warehouse where they had been stored for a quarter of a century. They brought them to Number One Garage at Headquarters Building. The case lingered on after that as a motion was put before the court declaring the slot machines contraband. Until a decision was made, the machines were once again in storage at the police property room

CHIEFS OF POLICE
Kansas City, Missouri
1874 to 2000

1.	Thomas M. Speers	04-15-74	05-04-95
2.	L.E. Irwin	05-04-95	11-27-96
3.	Henry S. Julian	12-16-96	04-07-97
4.	Thomas N. Vallins	04-07-97	08-27-97
5.	John Hayes	08-27-97	01-31-06
6.	Leo E. Koehler	01-31-06	02-15-07
7.	Daniel Ahern (Acting Chief)	07-31-07	08-09-07
	Ahern appointed Chief of Police	08-09-07	04-17-09
8.	Frank F. Snow	04-07-09	07-08-10
9.	Wentworth E. Griffin	07-09-10	06-23-13
10.	H.W. Hammil	06-16-13	06-06-17
11.	Thomas P. Flahive	05-04-17	06-26-18
12.	Larry A. Ghent (Acting Chief)	06-26-18	09-16-18
13.	Scott Godley	09-16-18	01-28-21
14.	Charles Edwards	01-28-21	08-15-22

15.	Frank H. Anderson (Acting Chief)	08-16-22	01-12-23
16.	Chester A. Vassar	01-12-23	12-31-23
17.	Paul V. Woolley	01-01-24	04-14-24
18.	William A. Shreeve	04-15-24	05-15-28
19.	Lincoln R. Toyne	05-15-28	03-14-29
20.	John Miles	03-15-29	04-24-30
21.	L.M. Siegfried	04-24-30	04-01-32
22.	Robert E. Phelan	04-01-32	10-01-33
23.	C.E. Reppert (Director of Police)	10-01-3	01-16-34
24.	Otto P. Higgins (Acting Chief)	01-16-34	04-14-34
	(Director of Police)	04-15-34	04-15-39
25.	Robert J. Coffey	04-15-39	07-11-39
26.	Lear B. Reed	07-11-39	09-30-41
27.	Harold Anderson	10-01-41	06-23-43
28.	Richard R. Foster	06-23-43	11-01-45
29.	Harold Anderson (second term)	11-01-45	02-19-47
30.	Henry W. Johnson	02-19-47	06-27-52
31.	Frank B. Collins (Superintendent)	06-27-52	07-10-52
32.	Bernard C. Brannon	07-10-52	04-19-61

33.	E.I. Hockaday (Assistant Superintendent, Missouri Highway Patrol) (Acting Chief)	04-19-61	08-28-61
34.	Clarence M. Kelley	08-28-61	07-09-73
35.	James R. Newman (Acting Chief)	07-10-73	10-31-73
36.	Joseph D. McNamara	11-01-73	10-04-76
37.	Marvin L. Van Kirk (Acting Chief)	10-04-76	01-01-77
	(Chief) – Van Kirk	01-01-77	02-07-78
38.	Norman A. Caron (Acting Chief)	02-07-78	12-31-78
	(Chief) – Caron	12-31-78	03-30-84
39.	Larry J. Joiner	03-31-84	06-15-90
40.	Steven C. Bishop	06-15-90	12-29-95
41.	Floyd Bartch (Acting Chief)	12-29-95	03-20-96
	(Chief) – Bartch	03-20-96	04-02-99
42.	Richard D. Easley	04-02-99	present

OFFICERS KILLED IN THE LINE OF DUTY

THE FOLLOWING TRIBUTE lists all Police Officers who have lost their lives in the line of duty. This page is dedicated to these brave Officers.

Martin Hynes 1881
Fred Houghton 1882
Patrick Jones 1892
John Martin 1892
Richard C. Fleming 1897
John E. Jacobson 1897
Joseph A. Zennetta 1901
Frank McNamara 1902
Alexander P. McKinney 1903
Stephen O. Flanagan .. 1903
Joseph P. Keenan 1903
Frank C. McGinnis 1904
William P. Mulvhill 1905
John Dwyer 1906
Albert O. Dulbow 1906
Michael P. Mulane 1908
Joseph Raime 1911
Homer Darling 1911
Robert I. Marshall 1912
Homer Riggle 1913
Andrew Lynch 1913
William F. Koger 1913
Bernard McKernan 1914

Samuel K. Holmes 1914
William Hauserman ... 1915
Glenn Marshall 1916
William A. Spangler 1916
John Houlehan 1916
Harris W. West 1917
Arthur M. Donetti 1917
Harry J. Keetling 1918
Michael Y. Sayeg 1918
Frank Mansfield 1918
Isaac Fenno 1919
Frederick F. Tierney 1919
Ula A. McMahan 1920
William H. Scobee 1920
James H. Horn 1920
Frank S. Archer 1920
William C. Bayne 1921
Carl J. Bicheti 1921
James N. Brink 1921
Gerald I. Fackert 1921
Richard P. McDonald .. 1922
Hershel M. Wyatt 1923
William C. Zinn 1923

Wellard I. Ferguson 1923
Wright D. Bryant 1923
Thomas J. Wilson 1923
Dennis J. Whalen 1924
Barney Jasper 1924
George E. Lawson, Jr. . 1924
Emmett C. Barnes 1924
Jack P. Wilcox 1924
Albert B. Cummings ... 1925
John V. Kincaid 1926
John W. Letter 1926
James H. Smith 1928
Ralph Hinds 1929
George R. Johnson 1929
Charles H. Dingman, Jr. 1929
Oliver P. Carpenter 1932
Richard E. Fitzgerald . 1933
Leroy Van Meyer 1933
William J. Grooms 1933
Frank E. Hermanson .. 1933
Morris Bigus 1933
Eric O. Bjorkback 1933
John Ruffolo 1934
William E. Wood 1934
Grant V. Schroder 1934
Frank Franano 1935
Frank Stevens 1936
William T. Cavanaugh 1936
Lawrence K. Morrison 1937
Thoman Mcauligge 1937
Henry Ships 1938
Ralph R. Miller 1941
Arthur J. Morris 1942
Melvon L. Huff 1946
James H. Owens 1947
Floyd M. Montgomery. 1948
Charles H. Perrine 1948
William S. Wells 1948
Charles W. Neaves 1948
Sandy W. Washington . 1948
Robert D. Edmands 1949
Clyde W. Harrison 1951
Mike Pearson 1954
William Kenner 1955
Richard Reeves 1957
Kieffer C. Burris 1960
Herbert E. Bybee 1960
Bennie A. Hudson 1960
Arthur J. Mart 1961
Richard L. Chaiborn ... 1962
Hugh L. Butler 1966
Marion P. Bowman 1966
George D. Lanigan 1968
Larry E. Oliver 1968
David C. Woodson 1968
Ronald D. Yoakum 1968
James W. Glenn 1969
Richard D. Bird 1969
John E. Dacy 1969
Robert W. Evans 1971
Russell D. Mesteagh ... 1975
Charles C. Massey, Jr. . 1975
Warren G. Jackman 1975
Douglas A. Perry 1978
John J. O'Sullivan 1978
David J. Inlow 1980
Phillip A. Miller 1983
Robert M. Watts 1990
James M. Leach 1992
Stephen A. Faulkner ... 1992
Jack S. Shepley 1992
Thomas R. Meyers 1998
Craig Shultz 2001

Photo Collage: Hugh Chase through the Years

Figure 135 — Hugh Chase through the years

Bibliography

Reed, Lear B. – **Human Wolves.** Kansas City, MO: Brown-White-Lowell Press, 1941

Kansas City Missouri 1808 – 1903. Whitney Vol. I, 1920

Burch, J.P. - **Charles W. Quantrell and His Guerrilla Band,** 1923

Dorsett, Lyle W. - **The Pendergast Machine,** 1968

Callahan, Clyde C. and Jones, Bryon B. – **Heritage of an Outlaw: the Story of Frank Nash,** 1979

White, Don – **The FBI Story.** New York, 1956

Shackleford, William Yancey, **Gunfighters of the Old West.** Girard, Kansas, 1943

Reddig, William M. – **Tom's Town.** Philadelphia: J.B. Luppincatt Co., 1977

Milligan, Maurice – **Missouri Waltz.** New York: Charles Scribners' Sons, 1948

Clayton, Merle – **Union Station Massacre.** New York: Bobbs-Merrell Co., 1975

Louderback, Lew – **The Bad Ones: Gangsters of the '30s and Their Molls.** New York: Fawcett, 1968

Unger, Robert – "Journal of a Massacre." **The Kansas City Times,** June 1983

Milligan, Maurice M. – **Missouri Waltz.** New York: Charles Scribner's Sons, 1948

Whitehead, Don – **The FBI Story: A Report to the People.** New York: Random House, 1956

Edge, L.L. – "Blood and Death at Union Station." **The Star Magazine,** June 17, 1979

Wellman, Paul I. – **A Dynasty of Western Outlaws.** Lincoln: University of Nebraska Press, 1966

Unger, Robert – **The Union Station Massacre: The Original Sin of J. Edgar Hoover's FBI.** Kansas City: Andrews McMeel Publishing

Illustrations: Retired Detective Bill Cronley

Acknowledgements

I wish to acknowledge the assistance given me in preparing this book by my mother Margaret Chase, my daughter Joli Anne Finke, my daughter Rebecca Stepp, my brother Dennis Chase, my sister Peggy Wood, and all the rest of my family for their contributions; and the following friends: Ms. Robin Meyers, Mr. James Funkhouser, Mrs. Catherine Stipe, Ms. Rosemary Stipe, Mrs. Deanne Korsak, Dr. D. Hassler, Ph.D., Ms. Barbara Hassler, Ms. Alice Boyd, Mrs. Janet Wornble, Mr. "Lucky" Mason, Ms. Dixie Weers, Mr. L.A. Edwards, Captain Lee O. Edwards, Retired Officer Jerry Price, the Staff of the Kansas City Missouri Library, and the Media Section and Retirement Unit of the Kansas City Missouri Police Department. My special thanks to the numerous Kansas Citians who lived through the 1920's and 1930's who allowed me to interview them as they remembered.